Praise for

WHY

"Over the last several years I've read quite a few books by thoughtful men and women about the lure of various forms of fighting. Josh Rosenblatt's *Why We Fight* is much the best of this mini-genre."
                                        —David Shields, author of *Reality Hunger*

"This is a terrific story—funny and scary and moving—as well as a thoughtful meditation on bravery, violence, pain, aging, and how getting hit in the face can change your life for the better."
                                        —Paul Bloom, Yale University, author of
                                        Against Empathy: The Case for Rational Compassion

"Fascinating. . . . A highly lucid, very personal meditation on selfhood . . . replete with a wide array of engaging literary and historical excursions—each of which gives the idea of fighting a dignity it might be harder to grant without."
                                        —NPR

"The thousands of hours Rosenblatt spent on the mat and in the ring attest to his passion and maniacal commitment to the bruising arts. He wasn't just aiming to produce this text—which nevertheless glistens with illuminations about courage and aging. The aim was self-transformation. Win or lose, it was mission accomplished."
                                        —*Wall Street Journal*

"A book worth reading not only for those who enjoy MMA and other forms of professional fighting, but for those who are baffled as to why such a bloody sport would ever be appealing."

—Salon

"A story of perilous becoming."

—Los Angeles Times

"Erudite."

—Publishers Weekly

"A very entertaining and informative chronicle of a quixotic journey of self-examination."

—Booklist

"By flirting with death in the metal cage, [Rosenblatt] achieves the transcendent experience of feeling truly alive. [He] offers much food for thought in this intellectual memoir blending sports and self-transformation."

—Library Journal

"'But I was tired of myself, so I said yes.' And thus begins Rosenblatt's journey from chicken to beast. I loved this book mostly for its gorgeous restraint. It ain't a macho brag but rather a piece of Old Testament prophecy—a clarion call advocating the importance of physicality."

—Chas Smith, author of *Welcome to Paradise, Now Go to Hell:*
A True Story of Violence, Corruption, and the Soul of Surfing

WHY WE FIGHT

WHY WE FIGHT

ONE MAN'S SEARCH
FOR MEANING INSIDE THE RING

JOSH ROSENBLATT

ecco

An Imprint of HarperCollins*Publishers*

A hardcover edition of this book was published in 2019 by Ecco, an imprint of HarperCollins Publishers.

FIRST ECCO PAPERBACK EDITION PUBLISHED 2020

Designed by Suet Chong

Library of Congress Cataloging-in-Publication Data has been applied for.

ISBN 978-0-06-256999-8 (pbk.)

20 21 22 23 24   LSC   10 9 8 7 6 5 4 3 2 1

For Katchen—straight down the line

We're more of the love, blood, and rhetoric school. We can do you blood and love without the rhetoric, and we can do you blood and rhetoric without the love, and we can do you all three concurrent or consecutive. But we can't give you love and rhetoric without the blood. Blood is compulsory.

—Tom Stoppard, *Rosencrantz and Guildenstern Are Dead*

WHY WE FIGHT

A BRIGHT NEW ROMANCE

The first time you get hit in the face you're overwhelmed with fear. Fear of the effect it will have on your body but mainly of how you're going to react. Will you cover up or run away or collapse or give up, or will you hit back? This question can be a lifelong torment, and one never knows the answer until the moment arrives.

The second time you get hit in the face you take offense. Now you know you can survive a punch, but you still feel instinctively protective of your body, convinced of its fragility, so you respond with indignation, like an animal protecting its young. Your face gets hot; the impulse to lash out is almost uncontrollable—the physical pain hurts less than the perceived slight.

The third time you get hit in the face you start to like it: you no longer fear the pain or your response to it and don't take it as a personal affront or worry that your body will collapse. You start to feel indestructible. You start to luxuriate in the life-affirming thrill of putting your body at risk and teasing death.

Soon you start to *love* getting hit in the face, and then you start to *need* getting hit in the face. You court danger now; life starts to feel empty without it. On bad days getting hit in the face triggers frustration, proof of your technical deficiencies and lingering bad habits as a fighter, even your failings as a human being. On good days getting hit in the face is a validation of your physical existence: *I am here; this is my swollen nose; this is my black eye; this is my aching jaw.* It pumps the blood faster through your veins; it makes your eyes water and your heart race. It makes the world shimmer. It reminds you of your mortality even as it snaps you into that concentrated present moment mystics call eternity.

Eventually you get used to getting hit in the face. It becomes just another thing you do, like brushing your teeth or getting the mail. Sometimes you find meaning there, sometimes you find nothing.

INTRODUCTION

It's nine o'clock on a Saturday morning in August and I'm hung-over and beaten up. Lying in bed, listening to the roar in my head and tracing the painful bump on the bridge of my nose that was just starting to form last night, I remember that yesterday, in a postfighting, endorphin-fueled moment of madness, I agreed to spar again this morning. I look at the clock. It's too late to back out now. I'd never hear the end of it. So, bent and bleary and very nearly broken, I drag myself out of bed.

The first thing I do is examine myself in the bathroom mirror to assess the damage I took last night, the result of a long sparring session with a strong but green partner who hasn't learned yet that enthusiasm is no substitute for technique and who throws all his punches out of hope and panic. Since wild punches thrown with great effort tend to come at you slowly, I had managed to avoid most of them, but near the end of our long session I started to tire and one of those huge punches slipped past my gloves and caught me square on the face, dazing me. My nose is now swollen and purple, the bruising spreading to the area under my left eye. I touch my upper cheek, and though it's tender, I know it won't be enough to get me out of sparring again today.

After a quick breakfast devoid of any of the flavors and fats and sugars that make waking up tolerable but that I have to deny myself now that I'm officially in training, I fill my gigantic gym bag, which still smells sour and sweaty from the night before, with three white T-shirts, an extra pair of gray running shorts, a pair of small mixed martial arts gloves, a pair of larger boxing gloves, a pair of kickboxing shin guards, a pair of bright red hand wraps (to make a single thumping unit of my fists and prevent my fingers and wrists from breaking upon impact with another human's skull), a state-of-the-art form-fitted mouthpiece (to protect my skull from the impact of another human's fists and shins), a jockstrap and protective cup, an enormous water bottle, and three towels. I throw the heavy bag over my sore shoulder and head out into the bright, muggy Brooklyn morning.

My walk to the subway station is long and goes entirely by way of a treeless street, and by the time I get there my shirt is soaked through. The subway car, of course, is freezing cold, sending a chill up my sweat-lined back, and after a twenty-minute ride I have another long walk, this time through a park in Greenpoint, a Polish enclave at the northwestern tip of Brooklyn long under siege from artists and musicians and other young people from neighboring Williamsburg. But no one—not Poles or hipsters—is in the park as I walk through. It's too early and too hot. Only mad dogs and the obsessed are on the streets this morning.

I walk into the gym and feel a familiar despondency. The great, cavernous room—a converted three-thousand-square-foot, two-story warehouse covered in thick mats and lined with punching bags—isn't air-conditioned, and it's ten degrees hotter inside than it is out. As a result, the room is nearly empty, just a few students in judo *gis* learning to throw each other to the ground as part of a Brazilian jiujitsu class in the far corner and one or two kickboxers punching the heavy bags that hang next to the boxing ring. Otherwise, the gym is uncharacteristically silent: no shouts from instructors, no hip-hop music blasting from the large speakers that hang in every corner. After dropping my bag from my aching shoulder with a groan, I lie down on one of the mats lining the floor and close my eyes. I can feel the residue of the whiskey and the fights from the night before overwhelming me. My nose throbs. My stomach is tentative. My head is foggy. All my muscles and joints seem tender. I could sleep right here. Maybe Anthony won't show up, I think. Maybe I'm off the hook. I let myself drift off for a happy moment. No, Anthony will be here. Anthony would never back out of a sparring session.

I need to get myself together. Despite having trained for less time than I have, Anthony has already fought three amateur mixed martial arts fights, and he trains with the zeal of the newly converted: at the gym for hours every day, long runs over the Brooklyn Bridge and back, god only knows what kind of byzantine dietary regimen he follows or how rarely he allows himself to be hungover. Meanwhile I'm forty years old, given to bouts of extreme physical degradation, and in training for only my first fight. Still, I have an advantage. For all his devotion, Anthony is small, probably four inches shorter and twenty pounds lighter than I am, and while it's important as a fighter to have skill, tenacity, athleticism, bravery, endurance, health, and luck, in the cage, size is destiny. The fact that I routinely beat Anthony when we spar says nothing about Anthony or me and everything about the cold realities of anatomy. He can hit me all he wants, I tell myself, and I will be fine. In fighting, you can't put a price tag on that kind of unearned biological confidence.

Generally, my rounds with Anthony unfold in accordance with the laws of physics (force = mass x acceleration) and tradition. I keep him far away with my jab and my kicks while he uses his speed to try and get in close, speed being the consolation nature grants smaller fighters. I poke at him, he rushes at me: we've been doing this dance for years. Today, though, something is different. Either Anthony's gotten better or I've gotten worse or I'm just as hungover as I thought I was, but I can barely lay a hand on him. He bobs and weaves and darts in and out, chipping away at me with his kicks, little slaps to my thighs and sides that don't hurt but that, taken together, aggravate, which is worse. Shots like these get in your head and cause you to react irrationally, like an animal swatting at a swarm of bees. Before I know it, I've abandoned technique (ten years of costly training) and I'm stalking Anthony around the ring like a wounded bear, lunging at him with wild punches that he's already moving away from by the time I've started to swing. Sensing my frustration, he starts throwing punches of his own at my face, all of which seem to land. Again, there's very little pain (even with his speed, Anthony only has so much mass to turn into force), only the rising swell of irritation and wounded pride.

Something primordial is taking me over, something deep down, something delusional and awful but undeniable—an urge to reestablish the proper order of things as I see them, to set the world right. Or maybe it's a lunging, leaping salve for my own wounded pride, I don't know. Whatever it is, I want to hurt Anthony and let him and everyone standing around the ring watching know that I'm not to be trifled with or chipped away at, that *I'm* the one with biology and Isaac Newton on his side. This is madness, of course: sparring-induced hysteria. I don't feel any real anger toward Anthony and have no actual desire to hurt him. He's just beating me up, and there's no point in looking for logic in the heart of a human being losing a fight.

Ten years ago, I never would have been in this position. Back then I was a devoted pacifist with a philosopher's hatred of violence and a dandy's aversion to exercise. I had never been in a fight, and I wore this fact proudly, as proof of my artistic and intellectual sophistication. Years of literary pursuits and cultivated irony had convinced me of the value of a cerebral/sensual life at the expense of the strenuous. I drank to excess, I smoked passionately, I ate indifferently, and I mocked any physical activity that didn't involve alcohol or nudity. Every night I got drunk in the hopes of discovering some new perspective or tumbling into a previously unimagined situation or finding my way into the bed of some new woman (even during those times when I claimed to be devoted to just one): all in thrall to the cult of the new and the quest for a thrill beyond the blandness and repetition of the everyday, of the predictable and domestic. I thought of myself as a libertine of the old school: proudly frail, a devoted observer, a decadent poet for whom the war on the body came through chemical means or not at all. I found the whole idea of violence tasteless and brutish, and I hated the thought of a fight breaking out anywhere—in a favorite bar or as part of a pay-per-view event on TV. To me, violence in any form was the shame of a species that refused to grow up and be civilized.

I came by my pacifism honestly. My father was an intellectual who taught me nothing about physical confrontation, hadn't even bothered—as fathers always seemed to do in the movies—to teach me how to make a fist. Most comfortable alone in a room full of books, leveled by depression that got heavier and bleaker the older he got, and plagued by near-heroic self-absorption and hypochondria (and with it a medicine cabinet full of painkillers, antidepressants, antihistamines, anti-anxiety pills, sleeping pills, heart pills, weight-loss pills, etc.), Joel Rosenblatt had gifted his only son a love of words but left him alone to figure out the physical realities of life himself. There were few backyard games of catch and no talks about the need for a man to stand up for himself. He was both brilliant and terrified, a scholar manqué living in a perpetual state of professional disappointment, growing more afraid of the world the smaller it got and the further he drifted from the life of the mind. I had always viewed my own avoidance of physical confrontation, my cowardice, as an inheritance, both a gift and a burden from a father who could never seem to give one without the other.

Still, deep down I knew there was some part of me that had always been attracted to the idea of fighting, no matter what I told myself or how terrified I was. There was violence buried deep in me somewhere, deprived but alive. I may have turned away from every fight on television, but I also stole glimpses over my shoulder. I may have run from every fight that had presented itself to me, but I was also dying to know what it was like to stick around, to hit and be hit, to harm and be harmed. I was horrified, but I was fascinated.

Eventually it became clear that if I hoped to complete my education in the senses, my resignation to the temptations of the body would have to move beyond sex and chemicals and make its way to violence. I needed to admit the connection between my lust for flesh and my lust for harming it. I saw, however faintly, that there were extraordinary sensations to be found in fighting. That pain was pleasure's reflection. That to fight would be to feel life *deeply*.

So, after more than thirty years of avoiding the issue, I set out to explore this dark world. And since mixed martial arts, which was then just barely knocking on the door of broad cultural acceptance, seemed to me like the height of civilization's shame and cultural collapse—fighting nonpareil—I figured I'd start there: in the depths.

And just like that, a long and distracting love affair was born.

Soon, time I used to spend watching classic movies, reading bleak novels, and cultivating meaningful human relationships was being filled watching videos of MMA fights and attempting to unpack their mysteries. One by one, all my assumptions about fighting and all my prejudices about fighters started to vanish. I witnessed tiny men triumphing over behemoths using little more than leverage, choking them into unconsciousness and forcing them to give up using mysterious arm locks whose secrets were beyond my understanding. I watched placid balding fighters with prominent love handles thrash terrifying, muscled, tattoo-covered gods with minimal effort and had all my assumptions about the relationship between the aesthetics of the human body and its fighting usefulness blown to pieces. Putting aside schoolyard terrors that live deep in the memory, I slowly got over my disgust of ground-and-pound, where one fighter sits on his opponent's chest and batters him with punches and elbows. I learned to stomach and then adore the techniques a lifetime of indifferent boxing viewing had taught me were barbaric, like dirty boxing, where a fighter punches his opponent while holding him in place behind the neck, and attacking someone who's been knocked to the ground.

I learned that the cage wasn't there just to sensationalize and titillate (though that, too; early designs featured an alligator-filled moat and an electric fence) but to prevent fighters struggling to gain dominant positions and work their way into submissions on the ground from tumbling out of the ring and into the crowd.

After learning about the brutal subtleties of Thai boxing I no longer recoiled in horror when one person kneed another in the face. Watching Brazilian jiujitsu masters at work convinced me that human beings had discovered a deeper understanding of the body and its vulnerabilities and a whole new world of physical possibilities. My notions of what could be done in a fight, and what a fight even was, were expanding, and instead of causing me to turn away in disgust, this expansion was pricking into life what would become a boundless fascination. I watched fighters covered in each other's blood hug each other like old friends. As the weeks and months went by, I could feel my fear and disgust drifting away, replaced by something bordering on obsession. Other sports I'd loved, like basketball and soccer, suddenly seemed bloodless and bland by comparison.

And the more fights I watched, the more I found myself wondering: How would I respond in that situation? After three decades of avoiding fights and rationalizing my fear as evidence of my refinement, I suddenly *needed* to know what I would do if someone hit me in the face, or worse. Would I run? Weep? Beg? Curl up and give in? Or were there reserves of courage and madness and self-destruction in me just waiting for the opportunity to show themselves? Was I man or mouse? Body or head? Blood or brains? Alive or dead?

When I was eight years old, an older boy punched me on the way home from school, and I responded by running away in hysterics. Though it was the only reasonable way to get to school from my house, I didn't take that road again for months, so terrified was I of this twelve-year-old blond menace with Coke-bottle glasses.

When I was fifteen, my friends and I were chased out of a McDonald's by another group of teenagers. One of them, we all swore later, was wearing brass knuckles, though this was never confirmed.

When I was eighteen, and an aspiring jazz drummer, I was hounded off the stage at a jam session in a bar in downtown Washington, D.C., by a tenor saxophonist who was angry at my inability to play fast enough to keep up with him. As I hurried out of the bar in shame, I heard him shouting over the crowd's laughter, "Fuck off, Ringo!" Cruelest of all jazz insults.

When I was twenty-one, I spent a summer in a small city in central Mexico. One Saturday night as I was sitting in the plaza smoking cigarettes and watching girls go by, a friend ran up in a state of panic. His face was flushed, his hair disheveled, his eyes wild. He told me he had just gotten into a fight at a bar down the street and was now being pursued by a small gang of men. Terrified, I told him to go to the cops, then I leapt into the first cab I saw and sped back to the safety of my hotel room, leaving my friend to face his fate alone.

When I was twenty-five, I lay on the floor of my mother's home in suburban Maryland one night hoping not to be noticed through the window by a group of rowdy, shirtless boys who were running around the neighborhood being teenagers. To this day I have no idea what I thought they'd do if they noticed me.

When I was thirty-one, I left my favorite bar rather than deal with a loud group of men with shaved heads and tattoo-covered arms who were smashing beer bottles and making a nuisance of themselves on the outside patio. I worried that at any moment they would turn their violence on me, so I went home and drank alone and hoped they wouldn't be there the next night, knowing I'd probably leave again if they were. I found out later that no trouble started that night and the men left not long after I did.

So much shame. A thousand beatings would have been better.

———

In the Book of Revelation, God condemns cowards to spend eternity in a lake of fire alongside the "unbelieving and the abominable, and murderers and whoremongers and sorcerers and idolaters, and all liars." In Dante's *Inferno*, cowardly souls are so universally loathed, they aren't even allowed into hell. They have to hover for eternity at its gates, barred from crossing the River Acheron, allowed neither in nor out, condemned for the sin of having no conviction, of living without "infamy or praise," of never really having been alive at all. "These of death no hope may entertain," Virgil tells Dante, urging him past the lowly band with their lamentations and moans, "and their blind life so meanly passes that all other lots they envy. Fame of them the world hath none, nor suffer. Mercy and Justice scorn them both." Cowardice drains the life out of human beings; it turns them into shadows and makes them contemptible and hateful, something we turn away from instinctually.

The fateful night when I realized I was going to make the leap out of mere voyeurism was a Friday in October. I was at a back-yard party in Austin, Texas, alternately boring and horrifying my friends with stories about some MMA fight I'd just watched, when a tall, rail-thin man walking by interrupted my sermon. He'd seen the fight I was recounting and was as eager to talk about it as I was. This was a crucial moment for me, one of the turning points in my biography, and I imbue it even today with an almost mystical resonance. Up until this point I'd either kept my newfound obsession with mixed martial arts a secret, so as not to upset the artists and intellectuals and progressives and humanists I surrounded myself with (and whom I counted my-self among), or, when I couldn't hold it in any longer, regaled them with stories while they sat by obligingly, barely tolerant of me and my new, bloody interest. But here, from out of nowhere, was a kindred spirit. Someone who understood me at last. My first fighting friend. Christian was a filmmaker and a writer and a good liberal ironist like me, but he was also a fight fan. And, just as important, he was a fighter. He had been training for years and had just recently become an instructor in the Israeli art of Krav Maga. He invited me to come to his gym and try a class, and in that fateful moment, cigarette in one hand and whiskey glass in the other, I knew I couldn't say no.

Christian's invitation came with a warning, though. Training was ruthless, he said, and not without its dangers. In fact, he had just recently gotten out of the hospital after suffering a terrible injury during instructor training, which consisted of a week at a gym in California with other teachers kicking and punching and kneeing and elbowing and choking and throwing and manhandling each other for eight hours a day, long past the point of exhaustion and into the realm of real risk, even trauma. In a fit of perhaps ill-advised courage, Christian had allowed himself to get kicked on the iliotibial tract, which runs the length of the outer thigh, hundreds of times over the course of a single day—gritting his teeth through the mounting pain and paralysis as an exercise in will. This was fine for his mind and his courage, he told me, but all of those kicks resulted in rhabdomyolysis, the release of dead muscle fiber into the bloodstream. One component of muscle fiber in vertebrates is an oxygen-binding protein called myoglobin, which, if it makes its way through the blood into the kidneys, can cause renal failure and even death. Thankfully, one of the other instructors in the class was a nurse. She took one look at the large black bruise quickly spreading over Christian's leg and convinced him to get to a hospital right away.

Because of a few kicks to the thigh and an overabundance

of pride, this man had nearly died, and now he was trying to convince me to come train with him. He's insane, I thought, he's absolutely insane. But I was tired of myself, so I said yes.

Jesus martyred himself when he was thirty-three, risking the pains of crucifixion and the torments of hell for a transformative experience. Dante was halfway through life when he decided that even the underworld would be preferable to spending one more second on the road he'd been walking. *I never saw so drear, so rank, so arduous a wilderness! Death could scarce be more bitter than that place!*

Midway through my life's journey, at thirty-three, no less, I had crashed into a wall of my own making. High living and hedonism had grown as repetitious and bland to me as the domesticity and quiet I'd been running from. Like any decent writer I'd managed to transform my vices and self-obsession into a philosophy and disguise my self-destruction as liberation, but I was exhausted by the prospect of more life, of an *entire* life, spent dodging the very terrors that had motivated me, however unconsciously, to do everything I had done up until that dreary point. Even your truest terrors and most troubling obsessions can become dull if you live with them for long enough. I knew that some kind of transformation, some new kind of experience would be better than the life I'd locked myself into. Even annihilation seemed preferable.

I decided to trade one fear for another. What had always frightened me most was violence and fighting, so I ran toward them, swapping perpetual, sublimated anxiety for the risk of sudden physical devastation. I decided to create a new life by brushing up against death.

"A time comes when you just have to forget what frightens

you most," Philip Roth wrote. This is self-re-creation as a shrug. No heroism, no romance, just recognition of the existential terror that is living and dying with the same miserable, nagging, insufferably stubborn anxieties tied around your neck, tormenting you one last time before they drag you down into the darkness. John Marcher, the protagonist of Henry James's "The Beast in the Jungle," spends his entire life waiting for the arrival of the catastrophe he's convinced he's fated to experience, only to discover in the end that the calamity he was doomed to suffer was the realization that he'd wasted his life waiting for it. *The Beast had lurked indeed, and the Beast, at its hour, had sprung.* I read that book when I was thirty, but it took me three years to really *feel* it.

Imrich Lichtenfeld, the creator of Krav Maga, grew up in Slovakia. His father, Samuel, a former circus performer and a detective in the police department, owned a gym in the capital city of Bratislava, and Imrich spent hours studying wrestling and boxing and gymnastics. He joined the Slovakian national wrestling team and when he was seventeen won the country's youth wrestling championship. The next year, 1929, he won the adult championship in both the light and middleweight divisions and also the national championship in boxing.

Following the rise of the Nazis in Germany in 1933 and the passage two years later of the Nuremberg Laws, which stripped Jews of German citizenship and prohibited them from marrying or having sexual relations with persons of German or related blood—committing "racial infamy," as the Nazis called it— attacks on Jews became common throughout Eastern Europe. Lichtenfeld and his friends had numerous altercations with anti-Semitic gangs in Bratislava. To improve their chances Lichtenfeld started developing a fighting style based on his knowledge of wrestling, boxing, judo, and karate and came up with a self-defense system built around a philosophy of simultaneous defense and attack; no-holds-barred tactics; and ruthless, overwhelming force. This system would form the basis of Krav Maga, from the Hebrew for "contact combat."

When I finally made the decision to learn to fight, though it was MMA I had fallen in love with, something primordial and ancestral drew me to Krav Maga. It called to me on a deeper frequency than mere curiosity. And how could it not? What assimilated, peace-loving, cerebral, ironic, good-natured, cowardly, lust-filled American Jew doesn't harbor violent revenge fantasies about Nazis?

Unlike MMA, Krav Maga has no value as a sport. Designed only to fend off murderous and incomprehensible malice, Krav forgoes all the niceties of athletic competition—like rules and sympathy—and declares anything done in the name of self-preservation fair game. Groin strikes, eye gouges, head butts, throat jabs, tearing, biting, thrashing, homicide: everything is allowed in Krav Maga. And every scenario is trained for, scenarios far beyond the bounds or imaginations of athletic competitions: surviving multiple attackers, fighting in cars and bars and on glass-strewn beaches, fighting off assailants armed with guns and bats, freeing oneself from hostage situations. From the reasonable to the ridiculous. Unlike Muay Thai and Brazilian jiujitsu lessons, Krav Maga classes are chaotic and primal, filled with screaming instructors and loud music and mass agitation and even weapons, meant to simulate the panic and adrenaline of violent situations and tap students into primal instincts and their darkest, often forever-dormant, passions.

By giving me a venue for these violent tendencies, Krav Maga introduced me to my bloodlust and animal aggression, which, as a law-abiding member of a civilized society, a loyal son of a pacifist father, and a lifelong devotee of inactivity and irony in response to hostility, I needed to access before I could even think about tinkering with the subtleties of particular techniques. If I had started my fighting education with Brazilian jiujitsu, which often feels like an intellectual exercise performed in thick pajamas, I wouldn't have lasted a week. It would have been one more cerebral puzzle in a life growing sick with them. But five minutes into my first Krav class I was learning how to knee another human being in the face and being encouraged to conjure rage while I did it. What a revelation! Like meeting some part of your personality you never even realized was there. Like seeing yourself in the mirror for the first time in all your tempestuous, primitive glory. In one of my early classes I marveled at the look of fury on the face of my partner, a quiet college professor, as he pounded on a bag with his fists as if he'd been overcome by a devil, his eyes bulging and his teeth flashing white, and I realized that must have been what I looked like three minutes earlier when I was the one clobbering the bag in a frenzy, howling and sweating and spitting and flailing wildly. To think I was capable of that! How right it felt to give in to my bloodiest instincts after all those cerebral, dormant, placid years, to feel my body fighting for its own preservation, to abandon my veneer of civilization and decency and experience the life-affirming thrill of putting my life, and the lives of others, at risk.

I soon found myself looking forward to getting punched in the head and choked into submission, and I started to recognize and long for the odd mixture of horror and envy that seemed to appear in people's eyes whenever I explained at a dinner party or the bar why I was limping or how I got this black eye or that broken finger. Any lingering fears I had of getting hit melted away with each training session. I could breathe: I was more man than mouse.

In 1940, after fending off Nazis with his fists for as long as he could, Imrich Lichtenfeld booked passage on one of the last ships to leave Europe with Jewish passengers during World War II. The stated destination of the ship was Paraguay, but it was actually bound for Palestine, in defiance of British immigration laws. The *Pentcho*, an old riverboat with a bad engine and a morphine addict for a captain, was denied entry into Romanian waters and shot at by Bulgarian troops, but somehow it made it all the way to the Aegean Sea before its boiler exploded and it was shipwrecked on an island in the Dodecanese chain, off the western coast of Turkey. Lichtenfeld, who nearly died from an ear infection during the journey, was able to find his way to Egypt, where he joined the Czech Legion fighting the Germans in North Africa. When he finally made it to Palestine, in 1942, he joined a paramilitary Jewish defense group and became an instructor in hand-to-hand combat, teaching what he'd learned on the streets of Bratislava to the members of what would in six years become the Israeli Defense Forces. By that point, though, the Jews were fighting Arabs, not Nazis, and the moral justifications behind Krav Maga had gotten murky.

Eventually it became clear that the nagging voice in my head that had been awoken by my first exposure to fighting wasn't satisfied with just training. Sparring and training were fine, but they were fakes and simulations. There was no real risk involved. The question was still there: What would I do in an actual fight?

I needed to know the answer to that question. I needed to

know the fear of walking into a cage, to know the sensation of being completely lost in a physical moment and the liberating thrill of complete transformation. I needed to know what it felt like to be that healthy, that strong, that simultaneously beaten up and impenetrable. I needed to know what it felt like to hit another human being in the face with ill intent. And I needed to get hit myself. *Truly* hit.

In 1923 Paul Gallico, a young New York *Daily News* reporter, approached heavyweight boxing champion Jack Dempsey with an idea for a story. New to the sports beat, Gallico worried that he couldn't write about boxing "graphically or understandingly" without having experienced it firsthand, so he asked Dempsey if they could spar. His only request was that the champion not aim for the body. "I explained that I expected to survive and said my only serious doubt was my ability to take it in the region of the stomach," Gallico wrote. "I asked the great man if he might confine his attentions to a less unhappy target." Dempsey obliged the journalist and knocked him out with "a good punch to the nose" in just over a minute.

"I can remember seeing Dempsey's berry-brown arm flash for one instant before my eyes," Gallico wrote about the experience. "Then there was this awful explosion within the confines of my skull, followed by a bright light, a tearing sensation and then darkness."

George Plimpton—the writer, actor, Manhattan socialite, and longtime editor of *The Paris Review*—took Paul Gallico's hands-on approach to sports journalism and made a career out of it, writing about what it was like to pitch against Major League Baseball stars in Yankee Stadium, lose thirty yards as a quarterback for the Detroit Lions, get trounced by Arnold Palmer on the golf course, and, like his mentor, box a former champion, in his case light heavyweight Archie Moore, who bloodied the writer's nose. He and Gallico shared what Plimpton called a "primal and tremendous curiosity with regard to sensation—to see 'what it was like.'" They were collectors of experiences.

But there's a difference between sensation and understanding, and a simulated experience has its limitations. Sure, it takes courage and curiosity to get into a ring with a professional boxer, but spending one round with Jack Dempsey isn't seeing what it's like to fight Jack Dempsey; it's seeing what it's like to get beaten up by Jack Dempsey for one round—which isn't what Dempsey's opponents were trying to do (even if that's what they often did). Plimpton once said that Paul Gallico had learned "all there was to know about being hit in the ring" by sparring with Dempsey, but there are plenty of people who spend entire lifetimes learning what it's like to be hit in the ring, so what's one round? Plus, Gallico's and Plimpton's journalistic experiments said very little about the ability to hit *back*, which, we can all agree, is half the game with fighting. Anyone with guts or madness in him can get hit by someone who knows how; it takes a different kind of madness, a more persistent kind, to stick around long enough to be one of the people who does the knowing.

1.

THE STRENUOUS MOOD

(ONE YEAR OUT)

Many mixed martial artists claim they experience something like bliss at the moment they lose consciousness from a choke. One practitioner says she once saw "shapes like mountains moving and pulsating with pink light" as she was passing out. Another says he was "flying through the woods like a bird." Still a third: "A great noise was inside my head, a great vibration. My whole body was moving in time with the vibration. There were sparks and colors everywhere, and the vibration seemed to open a huge hole in the earth."

These descriptions of bliss may read like pure poetry, but they will sound familiar to scientists who study near-death experiences. A 1982 Gallup poll found that 32 percent of NDE survivors reported feelings of peace and painlessness while hovering between this world and the next. Out-of-body experiences are common as well. Doctors have numerous theories to explain these phenomena, but that's all they are. Some point out that oxygen depletion in the brain can cause hallucinations. Others propose that a sense of spatial disorientation is caused by damage to the brain's temporoparietal junction, which is responsible for assembling data sent by the senses and organs into a coherent perception of one's body. Neuropsychologist David Carr believes the counterintuitive feelings of peace, pleasure, and calm some experience at the moment of death might be caused by morphinelike chemicals, such as endorphins and enkephalins, that are secreted by the brain when it's being depleted of oxygen. Others argue that the opioids triggered by the brain during a near-death experience are the same as those triggered in animals when they're under attack. It's as if the body, acknowledging just how difficult life is, generously provides us chemical relief at its end.

Seeking a less-scientific explanation for the mysteries of the world, Tibetan Buddhists—death obsessives who are taught to meditate on the subject morning, noon, and night—speak of the bardo, an intermediate realm between this life and the next, between states of consciousness. Skilled meditators experiencing the chikhai bardo, or "bardo of the moment of death," come face-to-face with the "clear light of reality" as they slip out of life and into death and then into their next rebirth. But even for the most enlightened and dedicated masters this luminosity only lasts a moment, like a grappler choked into unconsciousness. The light is just a glimmer of something in the corner of your eye.

My first real brush with death comes not long after I make the decision to fight, the perfect initiation into my fraught new reality. This lesson is delivered one cold January evening by a mixed martial arts coach named Jake, a New York City native and longtime professional fighter.

During a long and bruising sparring session, Jake sweeps my feet out from under me and tosses me to the ground, crawls onto my back, and catches me in a rear naked choke. The rear naked choke is among the first things you learn in Brazilian jiujitsu. The aggressor shoots one arm under the chin of his opponent from behind, brings his forearm back up against the side of the neck, and grabs onto his own shoulder. His free arm then presses down on the neck from behind the head, creating a vise, squeezing his opponent into unconsciousness. In response to being caught in this vise I flail around and struggle to loosen Jake's grip around my neck like I was taught, to peel his feet from the inside of my thighs to get some space, to turn on my side to relieve the pressure and pop my hips out, but it's no use. Escaping a rear naked choke is hard enough in the best circumstances. When the person applying the choke is a lifelong professional fighter and you're just an aging hopeful in the throes of a delusion, escape is a fantasy.

There are two kinds of chokes in MMA: the blood choke, which impedes blood flow from the heart to the brain, and the asphyxia choke, which obstructs airflow, usually by compression of the windpipe. The rear naked choke is a blood choke. At first it causes compression of the external jugular vein, which runs down the side of the neck, hindering the flow of blood from the head to the heart. Eventually the pressure narrows the carotid artery, which is the primary source of blood back to the brain. If the choke is applied low enough on the neck the vertebral arteries, which run alongside the cervical spine in the back of the neck, are also compressed, causing cerebral hypoxia: deprivation of oxygen to the brain. The face of the person caught in the choke gets flushed, her vision starts to fail, her blood pressure falls, blood supply to the brain gets cut off, and within seven to ten seconds she loses consciousness. Doctors can't say with any accuracy when the hallucinations begin.

Doctors *can* say that any serious risks from a blood choke are generally minimal because it takes four to six minutes of constricted blood flow and oxygen deprivation, called anoxia, before permanent damage to the brain is likely to occur. Still, this is MMA, so there are always risks. In the case of a rear naked choke: short-term memory loss, hemorrhaging, even retinal damage. Occasionally you hear about some poor soul in a gym somewhere suffering a stroke after going unconscious. You might even think about him for a few quiet seconds as you wrap your hands before a sparring session. But you long ago resigned yourself to the risks.

I know the risks going into my sparring session with Jake, of course, but I'm not prepared for the intimacy of our encounter. Sparring is supposed to be an impassive affair, as unemotional as you can manage. Jake is the one always drilling this into our heads, in order to promote control and civility and prevent the injuries that are bound to occur when two people throwing punches at each other give in to their most ungovernable passions. Jake is always admonishing us to go lighter, to "have a conversation," even to avoid looking each other in the eyes, because once the eyes flare up in the face of a man you're fighting, primordial instincts take over and short-circuit your sense of camaraderie and decency. Sparring, Jake always says, is not fighting.

I'd like to think I'm good at honoring that distinction and at controlling my emotions. The few times I've had the privilege of sparring with Jake (there's a great egalitarian streak that runs through the mixed martial arts world: if you train at a gym where a UFC champion trains and you stick around long enough, chances are you'll one day have the chance to spar against him or her; this is roughly the equivalent of going to the YMCA and playing a game of one-on-one basketball against LeBron James), I've performed with admirable dispassion. True, he hit me with nearly every kick and punch and throw he attempted, while I stumbled and lurched around him, but we always sparred with a calm and pleasant mutual respect, even if just under the surface I was boiling with rage and disappointment.

But tonight something bad is in the air, something corrosive that isn't supposed to be there. With the first punch I throw it's as if I've released something in Jake, some darkness that has been waiting and feeding upon itself, some depression, some un-named weight.

There's malice in the punches and kicks Jake throws and in the clinches he wraps around my neck. In the slicing elbow that whizzes by my head, missing my nose by an inch—a warning shot. In the repeated knees to my midsection that knock the wind out of me and the dismissive, even disrespectful way he sweeps my feet out from under me with his own and tosses me to the ground over and over. In the chokes and the armbars when we are down on the floor. And there is malice in the rear naked choke he uses to nearly strangle me unconscious and drag me toward bliss. His punches are like nothing I've ever felt before. Each one seems to freeze my nervous system for a moment. They scramble my brain and shake my body, and they put me in mind of my fragility and my mortality.

Jake tells me after our round is over that he was just beating me up for the sake of enlightenment, to teach me some technical lesson I wasn't getting. He assures me his motivations were pure, even noble, but I sense something different. I've been thinking over the last few months that any affection Jake once had for me has vanished. I don't know why exactly—Did I say something? Did I do something? Or was it just incompatible personalities finally acknowledging their incompatibility after a hopeful grace period?—but whatever the case, it's undeniable: Jake has ceased to like me, and, under the spell of one of his many black moods, he decided, consciously or not, to punish me for it.

In his lectures on saintliness published in 1902, the psychologist William James said, "When the strenuous mood is on one, the aim is to break something, no matter whose or what. Nothing annihilates an inhibition as irresistibly as anger does it; for, as Moltke says of war, destruction pure and simple is its essence." Tonight the strenuous mood was on Jake, as was an irresistible anger.

Helmuth Karl Bernhard Graf von Moltke, the German general and war philosopher, wrote in his 1871 essay "On Strategy" that "no battle plan survives contact with the enemy." One hundred years later, Mike Tyson updated that sentiment for the ring: "Everyone has a plan until they get punched in the mouth." That's how I felt sparring with Jake. All the art I thought I'd cultivated in myself over the previous years of training and sparring vanished the first time I took a real punch in the face from a real fighter, and all my strategizing was cut off as quickly and as completely as the blood trying to get to my brain. I'd been on the losing end of countless sparring rounds, but this was the first that felt perilous and personal.

But things aren't supposed to get personal when we spar. We aren't supposed to let our emotions get away from us. That's what Jake told us. And no matter how bizarre it seemed to me to try and separate violence from the passions, I trusted him—me the loyal acolyte: *Mine not to make reply / Mine not to reason why / Mine but to do and die.* So I tried to separate sparring from its darkest moorings and the desires inside me. I tried to buy into Jake's philosophy that fighting should be thought of the same way we think about basketball and baseball and tennis—sports that don't cultivate a direct line to our most primal and terrifying instincts. Jake told me what makes a fighter is what makes any other athlete: strength, will, desire, discipline, self-denial, hard work, persistence. He lined up all the clichés. But all I could think was: What about madness? What about anger? What about self-destructiveness and delusion? What about desperation? What about malice? What about fear and self-doubt? What about lingering trauma? What about masochism and cruelty? What about the violence deep down in the blood of the species, bucking against civilization and decency?

The truth is, I can't count the number of times I've allowed myself to indulge in personal animus during sparring sessions. I don't know how not to. And I'm not convinced I shouldn't. Every time I manage to get the better of someone who has always gotten the better of me, every time I trade punches and kicks with someone more talented or stronger than I am, every time I toss an opponent and watch him topple through the air, every time I prove to my partner that I won't be allowing my cowardice to take me over, every time I don't break and she doesn't break and we both get some strong shots in on the other and we walk away with each other's respect and some of each other's blood, I feel a thrill impossible to simulate with unemotional, dispassionate, clinical sparring. This thrill goes beyond technique and self-control. There's something primordial there, something down in the blood.

A hundred years ago, a wave of anti-Semitic madness swept through Eastern Europe like fire, a mass psychosis, a communal hysteria. Riots touched off in Warsaw and Odessa and Prague and Chernigov and Yelizevetgrad and a thousand tiny villages and small cities in between. Thousands of Jews were murdered by mobs. Entire towns were burned to the ground. Soldiers killed women and children. In the small town of Kishinev on Easter Sunday 1903, gangs of Ukrainian citizens, driven into a frenzy by local priests and anti-Semitic newspapers, descended on the Jewish community, killing men and women, even tearing babies apart with their bare hands. "At sunset," the *New York Times* reported, "the streets were piled with corpses and wounded." My great-grandmother was ten years old when the pogroms came to her hometown of Kamenetz-Podolsk. She saw the madness in gentile eyes. So Esther Kornbluth, who grew up in a house with a floor made of goat dung, left her home and made her way to Hamburg, Germany, where she boarded the SS *President Lincoln* bound for America. In Brooklyn, she met her future husband, my great-grandfather, who had run from his own nightmare in Burshtyn, a shtetl in western Ukraine just 115 miles from Kamenetz-Podolsk. Thirty years after Isidore Kriegsfeld's escape to America, the Nazis cleared out the entire Jewish population of Burshtyn and gunned them down in the nearby city of Rohatyn. All of my great-grandparents had stories like this.

My gym is located in one of the biggest Eastern European neighborhoods in Brooklyn, so I often spar with fighters from Russia and Ukraine and Poland. They tend to be big, stern, unsmiling men, with crew cuts and muscular arms and pale tattooed skin. And every once in a while, when a peculiar mood strikes me, I allow myself to contemplate the history of my people and the history of theirs and fold my contemplations into our sparring sessions. Before our rounds start, I look at them and think: "That's what they looked like. The men who burned down my great-grandmother's village and murdered my great-grandfather's neighbors, the soldiers who let it happen or joined in. *I know those faces.*" And I allow myself to believe that the men I'm sparring with are somehow responsible for their ancestral past and that I'm somehow responsible for mine. I see something deep in the visage of their race and feel something deep down in the blood of my own.

When I'm in this mood, sparring sessions become historical purging sessions, attempts at metaphorical reclamation, even if my opponents don't know it (and how could they?). Something hereditary is roused, and I'm overcome by conflicting but equally overpowering instincts: fear and murder, cowardice and hate. Each kick they throw seems heavy with significance; every punch I land feels like revenge. Hopped up on adrenaline and fear and righteousness, in the throes of all that lustful violence—yes, lustful—I descend into a kind of madness. When my forbears saw gentile Russians and Poles, they saw orgies of rage and inhumanity and the terror of the mob. Can you blame me, then, when I'm in the middle of a simulated trauma like sparring, for tapping into a great ancestral anxiety?

Of course you can. It's insanity to think this way. The men and women I spar against are sweet and decent, without any anger in them, certainly not for me as a Jew. They don't deserve to bear the sins of their fathers. They might not even be aware of them. Plus, we're all Americans now, freed from the weight of our collective pasts. Still, I feel a strange retributive responsibility when I spar with them, as if I need to vindicate my people. It's ridiculous, I know, but this impulse comes from collective blood memory. And everything in fighting comes back to blood: spilled blood, blood chokes, ancestral blood. *Blood, blood, blood.*

In classical Greek medicine, blood was associated with air and light and spring, and with a merry, gluttonous, and lustful personality. In his most famous work, *Natural Magic,* published in 1558, the Italian scholar Giambattista della Porta, known as the Professor of Secrets, wrote that those of a sanguine temperament are "loving, liberal they, loving the laugh and song. And strong they are, and passing brave." Those filled with blood are truly alive, shrinking from neither fear nor indulgence.

When Dante comes across the first group of sinners suffering just inside the gates of hell in the *Inferno,* he is told by his guide that they are "abject cowards who had never lived," who are being punished for neither keeping faith with God nor rebelling against him. These poor souls are condemned to suffer through eternity the incessant stings of "monstrous flies and wasps that swarmed about them, making their faces run with streams of blood that, mingled with their tears, in slimy pools lay round their feet." The blood that comes from the bodies of those incapable of true life is wan and watery, the very opposite of the sanguine "liquor of life" in all its vitality. Maybe the fear of shedding blood in public stems from this shared cultural instinct, from an ancient, inherited belief in blood's personality-revealing properties: the unconscious sense that anyone who sees our blood will know what kind of person we are. The fear of blood is the fear of seeing evidence of our cowardice and insignificance.

In East Asian cultures, if a man gets a bloody nose he is assumed to be experiencing sexual desire. The Cherokee believe menstrual blood is a source of female strength and has the power to destroy enemies. According to Scandinavian folklore, when the hero Hjalti drank the blood of a wolf, "his courage increased, his strength waxed, he became very strong, mighty as a troll, [and] all his clothes burst open." In blood is life and vitality.

Shame is in the blood, too. Like my shame over the thought that my people didn't do enough to defend themselves, in Kishinev or Odessa or Auschwitz, that they were complicit in their own destruction. That I come from a long line of victims. This must explain, at least in part, my fascination with fighting—the desire to right great historical wrongs and redeem an entire unhappy people by putting on gloves and shin pads and lashing out at the modern-day sons of Russia in a gym in Brooklyn. To replace their cowardice with my combativeness. Ancestral reproach through self-delusion.

After hearing about the Easter pogrom in Kishinev, the Ukrainian Jewish poet Chaim Bialik wrote "In the City of Slaughter" to lament his people's "passivity" in the face of the mobs:

> Let me lead you to all the hiding places
> The shit houses, the pig stalls, and all the crowded places
> And you will see with your own eyes where your brothers
>   were hiding.
> Your brothers, your people, the sons of the Maccabees,
> The great grandchildren of the lions, the seed of the
>   saints!
> Twenty souls in one hole!

Those who praised my name and sanctified my honor
They escaped like mice and hid like fleas!
And they died like dogs and
In the morning they were found.

But I'm not from Minkowitz or Burshtyn or Kishinev. And
I'm not dead. I'm a freeborn American man, alive and well, a
Jew in the land of our long-awaited redemption. Not Israel,
no—Brooklyn. So I'll fight the Russians *here* and we'll all shake
hands and clap shoulders and smile at one another when we're
through, and here in Brooklyn is where I'll forgive them for their
ancestral past and rid myself of these poisonous notions about
my own and drop the weight of history from my shoulders. Like
a true American.

Who knows? Maybe ideas like these, however unconscious, were
in Jake's head tonight. Maybe I stirred up some ancient, inherited discontent in him, something I couldn't see and even he
couldn't recognize. Maybe I reminded him of someone or something deep in his blood. Maybe that's why he beat me up and laid
me low. And if that's true, who am I to be mad at him? Who am
I to judge a man for letting his emotions get the better of him in
a fight?

Besides, the experience was edifying. Forty years into life
I had caught my first real beating. My first in the gym, on the
streets, in a bar, anywhere. And I lived to talk about it. For
the first time I truly felt the fragility of my hold on life. I didn't
have any hallucinations, like the Tibetan Buddhists with their
bardo or the Brazilian jiujitsu students drifting into poetry, and I
experienced no overwhelming sense of bliss. But when I realized
I was sparring with a man who could kill me, I did have a revela-

tion. I saw what this world I'd entered into was really about, and what kind of primal forces I was messing around with. Forces of death and destruction and dark mystery. Ten years into this experiment in violent self-re-creation, I was finally understanding the madness at its heart.

2

THE GREAT FEAR

(TEN MONTHS OUT)

For more than a decade, Peter Storm has been putting on illegal MMA fights in New York City. Storm's Underground Combat League events are legendary among the very small group of local fight fans who know about them: half legitimate sporting shows, half unlicensed circuses that are always in danger of being shut down by the police or collapsing into chaos. Over the years, UCL events have taken place all over the city, wherever Storm can manage to talk himself in the door: boxing gyms in Brooklyn, warehouses in Queens, even a mosque in the Bronx, where, legend has it, a terrified fighter was once replaced on the card at the last minute by a member of the audience who quickly found himself in a submission hold he had no idea how to get out of, and soon after that with a broken leg.

Evidence of this shambolic spirit is everywhere at UCL events. The referee hasn't been sanctioned by the New York State Athletic Commission. The official timekeeper's only qualification seems to be that he owns an iPhone. The closest thing to a ring doctor the promoter provides is cab fare to the hospital. More than one fight has been canceled because a fighter was picked up on a parole violation, and nearly every event I've ever attended has ended with the threat of violence spilling out of the ring. One title fight I'd been waiting months to see was called off at the very last minute after the challenger accused the champion of missing weight. That the challenger, Peter Storm, was also the event's promoter and weigh-in official struck the champion as a conflict of interest, so he threw his belt into the ring in protest, hurled a mountain of insults at anyone within earshot, and stomped off into the street with his coaches and friends. Storm and his team followed behind him screaming and shouting, and for about twenty minutes it looked like the fight would take place right there on 171st Street. But in the end it was just a battle of words.

The fighters at Underground Combat League events are as diverse as the city they come from, some highly trained amateurs looking to test themselves before moving into the embrace of legal legitimacy across the Hudson River in New Jersey, others newcomers taking their first tentative steps into competitive fighting, and the rest untrained brutes who just want to try their luck or stave off boredom. I've watched professional bouncers fight alongside teenagers, dentists, college wrestling coaches, and psychopaths. Unlike at sanctioned shows, these fighters aren't required to provide blood samples or medical documents, and judges aren't required to be trained. But what UCL fights lack in legitimacy and morality, they make up in passion and desperate longing: a spirit of abandon and deviance that can only exist outside the law. There's something honest about such an approach to MMA promotion, an admission that fighting isn't just a sport but something much darker as well.

In just a few hours, though, it will all be gone. After today's fights Peter Storm's Underground Combat League will be swept into the dustbin of MMA history. And something beautiful will be lost forever.

Back when the UCL was born, MMA was illegal in New York State, part of the inevitable backlash against the sport that took place in the late 1990s, a time of hand-wringing and moral panic during which politicians, parents' groups, and religious organizations decided that cage fighting, which had appeared just a few years earlier, was too much for American civilization to bear. So Storm stepped into the void, defying the law and the moralists to bring mixed martial arts back to New York City. And for years his was the only show in a town that for much of the twentieth century had been the center of the fighting universe, the city where Rocky Marciano knocked out Joe Louis and Muhammad Ali got his revenge on Joe Frazier.

But in March 2016, the New York State Legislature at last came to its collective senses and voted to make mixed martial arts legal again, the last state in the union to do so, opening the door to rules and regulations and all the other niceties that turn fighting into sport. And so, starting tomorrow, Peter Storm's job— keeping MMA alive in the world's greatest, and most squeamish, city—will be no more.

But for the next few blessed hours, before the legislators and regulators and athletic commissions step in to tie New York MMA into a neat, safe little package, we still have the UCL in all its inspired, lawless glory. And here at this old boxing gym in the Morris Heights section of the Bronx, with Peter Storm in his traditional blue judo *gi* announcing the fights, with little kids wandering around eating snacks while fighters barely older than they are risk their lives, with each fight starting not with the sound of a bell but the referee telling the fighters to "fuck each other up," all is right with the world.

———

In the first fight of the last UCL show ever, a young man named Steven, tall and muscular and imposing, with a pale broad hairless chest covered in a *Mars Attacks* tattoo, belies his size and strength and gets pummeled for three rounds by a much smaller, much softer opponent. This is because Steven spends the entire fight with his hands down and his chin up. Protecting your chin is the first rule of defensive fighting, but a fighter's understanding of that often goes out the window the first time he takes a real punch to the face from someone who is trying to hurt him. One good hit landed with hostility can wipe the memory clean.

Throughout the fight Steven and his opponent grab onto each other and throw wide, slow, looping punches and make desperate leaps at takedowns, exhausting themselves. By the time the third round begins they can barely stand. A minute in they nearly tumble through the ropes in each other's arms and go crashing headfirst into the large window the ring has inexplicably been placed right next to. Thankfully, the fighters react in time and pull each other back onto the canvas, where they collapse in a heap, sparing us the horror of watching them smash through the window and fall two stories onto Jerome Avenue below, to die under the elevated tracks of the 4 train. Call it an MMA miracle.

Eventually, Steven succumbs to his inadequacies. He has heart and muscles but doesn't know how to use them. Not long after the two men recover from their near brush with death and pull themselves back to their feet, Steven gets thrown to the ground once more, and this time he seems to have had the will to fight back drained out of him. He curls his knees up to his chest and wraps his head in his hands while his opponent swarms him from the top with great thundering punches that come in wide arcs from behind his back. Despite his size, Steven suddenly looks like a child, seeming to grow smaller with each punch that lands, and the audience grows unsettled waiting for the fiasco to end, sympathetic to the sight of a grown man in regression and wincing at the sound of each *thwack* as it echoes through the gym. It's really the sounds at these smaller fights and not the sights that conjure the physical immediacy of violence: there's something intuitively repulsive and magnetic about the sound of flesh hitting flesh. The cheering, so prominent twenty seconds ago, has stopped, replaced by silence and the occasional cry to stop the fight. These are the moments that make even hardened fight fans wonder about themselves: What is wrong with *me* that I can love something like *that*?

When the referee finally calls off the fight, it's an act of mercy, and we can breathe again. Some sense of humanity has been restored to our dirty little world. Steven's face is a mess of blood and confusion, but he's able to stand up on his own. We applaud both men, and the loser raises a defiant fist as if to say, *Defeated, yes, but still alive!* Still, for all his courage and strength, this young man has no business fighting—no business, that is, beyond the God-given right to thumb his nose at death.

Most of the fights at today's event unfold like this: fighters winging wild punches and crashing into each other before collapsing from fatigue. And all the time the crowd is shouting advice from the makeshift stands, calling out for the fighters to bob and weave and duck and tuck their chins and move their feet and perform the 101 other tactical maneuvers every young fighter knows but few remember once the bell rings and there's a man standing fifteen feet away with malice in his heart.

Usually this advice doesn't amount to much, just the outbursts of spectators caught up in the thrill of bloodlust and hoping to convince those around them that only they are in possession of the true and holy fighting knowledge, not the man in the ring or his coaches, and surely not the other spectators. Sometimes, though, these opinions are indisputable and instructive. During one fight, a man sitting behind me in the makeshift stands, fed up with watching glorified bar brawls but forced to suffer again as two young tattoo-covered Latino bantamweights lunge at each other like elementary school kids on the playground, artlessly, with chins up, eyes shut, arms windmilling madly, not a fake or a feint or a setup in sight, as if, despite the presence of their coaches and their gym T-shirts, they've never trained a day in their lives—finally this man, clearly a lover of boxing but finding no sweet science anywhere in that west Bronx gym, can stand the chaos no longer, and during a quiet moment, after the fighters have once again grasped on to each other following a wild and meaningless exchange of punches, he shouts, "Someone *please* throw a fucking jab!" It's like a cry for mercy from a penitent, full of desperate passion, and it echoes through the gym. I turn in my chair and give him a smile of recognition, but his appeal goes unanswered. Manic energy is having its way with technique.

There are two areas of the brain that are called upon when a potential danger appears. The ancient amygdala is part of the brain's limbic system and deals with primitive processes, like emotion and fear and aggression, and the initial evaluation of potential threats. The much younger prefrontal cortex is the part of the brain associated with the higher functions, like reason and decision-making, that distinguish humans from other animals. When faced with a potential threat, the amygdala sends messages to the prefrontal cortex, which then analyzes them to determine the nature and severity of the threat. If the prefrontal cortex determines no threat is there, it will send a message back to the amygdala and shut down its response.

When these two systems determine that danger is real, the sympathetic nervous system takes over. The SNS is one half of the autonomic nervous system, an ancient part of the body responsible for regulating its unconscious actions and producing the symptoms of arousal. During a fight-or-flight situation the SNS focuses all the body's resources on struggle, flooding the bloodstream with adrenaline (the hormone that governs the brain's fight-or-flight response), pounding the heart to pump blood faster, opening sweat glands, sending pain-deadening chemicals into the brain, drying the mouth, preparing the whole organism to protect itself.

How well the amygdala and prefrontal cortex communicate with each other determines how the brain and the body will react to potential danger and fear. A balance is required to keep the host both alive and free from unnecessary panic, to allow it to control fear without being swamped by it. An active amygdala under stress stimulates a region of the brain stem called the locus ceruleus to send noradrenaline to the prefrontal cortex, which becomes more active and focused. An overactive amygdala, uninhibited by the rationality of the prefrontal cortex, can cause the whole system to malfunction by sending frantic messages to the prefrontal cortex that will shut down that system's ability to engage in rational thought. Fine motor skills will vanish, hearing will decrease, vision will narrow. Eventually panic will set in.

Don't blame the fighters, in other words. This energy is stronger than they could hope to be. It arrives with all the inevitability of death. Anyone fighting for the first time—not sparring but fighting: in front of a crowd, half-naked, against a stranger whose intentions and capacities and psychological state are unknown—will be consumed and eventually undone by it. And all the training in the world can only hold it back for a moment or limit the damage it does.

Not long after the event in the Bronx, I went to watch a few of my sparring partners fight their first-ever fights in the lobby of a former bank in Manhattan's lavish Financial District, done up in Classical Revival style. Unlike the Underground Combat League, this was a legitimate, sanctioned event. There were judges and doctors and licensed referees and athletic commission officials and wandering beer vendors and a small squad of rail-thin, buxom ring-card girls—everything you could ask for from a prizefight. Twenty yards from the ring, teammates of the men and women fighting stood and craned their necks to see around the enormous mosaic columns blocking their view of the ring, most wearing T-shirts with the names of their fight gyms emblazoned on them, which strained against great biceps and shoulders and chests. Ringside, meanwhile, sat rows of soft Wall Street bankers and stockbrokers, looking for a little amusement at the end of a long workweek, their hair thick with pomade and button-down work shirts worn loose at the collar, rolled up at the sleeves, and stretching over paunches. We were eight miles and a world away from the poverty of Jerome Avenue and the lawlessness of the Underground Combat League.

But despite this dramatic difference in setting and aesthetic, the same force, the same sense of chaotic abandon and fear, that ruled the first-time fighters that Sunday afternoon in the Bronx had its way with every young fighter that Friday night in lower Manhattan as well, turning my well-bred, well-trained, well-disciplined teammates into brutes.

At the gym these fighters were all budding artists, young and fearless and technically sound and bursting with confidence. When we sparred together they would often overwhelm and delight me with their speed and prowess, making up for disparities in size and strength by relying on composure and technical acumen. Jon, small but fast, would dance around me with dazzling footwork, constantly switching stances from left to right and back again, moving in and out of range before I could get a glove on him, always slipping in a jab or an inside leg kick as he exited. Michelle would throw body kicks that seemed to pop from out of nowhere and then follow them up with push kicks that would prevent me from making any advances in return, stopping my counterattacks and driving me mad. And David, the genius of the group, would engulf me with aggression, throwing fakes and feints and jabs that transformed magically into hooks midpunch, leaving me frozen in place and my head throbbing, and then he would dive away again, kicking me in the midsection for good measure, reminding me: *I can do this any time I want.*

Then fight night came and all that art and discipline, all that genius, was swallowed up in a rush of fear and adrenaline, like a sailboat swamped by a great wave. Gone were Jon's speed and quickness and subtle footwork, replaced by huge static haymaker punches and desperate kicks that missed their target or crashed into his opponent's arms and shins harmlessly while sapping Jon of his energy. Michelle pushed jabs out at her opponent's face but stood upright and kept her own chin way too high and got hit repeatedly on the face by her opponent's right-hand counters. Her normally lightning-fast kicks were tentative and plagued by doubt. Over and over again we screamed for her to attack with abandon, to remember herself, but it was no use: there was no hatred in her. David's bruising style was a better fit with the chaotic inevitabilities of a first fight, but even he reverted to his most brazen and bashing animal instincts once the bell rang, forgetting his head movement and the hypnotic bolo punches that whirled close to your body before crashing into your chin, or whirled close to your chin before crashing into your body, replaced by an aesthetic of overwhelming force and volume.

All these brilliant young fighters I admired so much sank one after the other into carnal rages or paralyzed passivity. They either exhausted themselves with misguided outbursts of energy or were drowned by anxiety. All the art and science and delicacy I had watched grow and develop in the gym for months was swept away in the rush of panic and the crowd. The energy claimed them all. Walking back to the subway that night I could come to no other conclusion than this: no matter what a fighter is in the gym, no matter how talented and technical and composed, when he takes off his shirt for the first time in front of two hundred people in a converted bank in lower Manhattan or a bowling alley in Hell's Kitchen or a dilapidated boxing gym in the Bronx, he goes suddenly and irretrievably mad.

There might be a lesson here for me if I have eyes to see it.

If surrendering to the Great Fear is how everyone reacts in a first fight, maybe, if I can tuck my own panic away just slightly during *my* first fight, maybe I can use this knowledge to my advantage. If I can just survive my opponent's first adrenaline-fueled burst of murderous, uncontained energy, keeping it at bay with my jab and eluding it with my footwork, if I can manage to stay outside the reach of the storm, if I can harness whatever tranquility of mind age brings and cling to it, then maybe I can pick my opponent apart with my technique. And then, when the adrenaline has subsided and he's exhausted and barely able to keep his arms up, that's when I'll make my move and have my way with him. This strikes me as a wise strategy, one built on recognition of shared humanity: a strategy with some real poetic and sociological imagination. And it might even work, as long as I can defy tradition and find a way to override my own terror.

In fighting class, instructors are always drilling us in the basics, working on the theory that once you're in the ring in front of all those people and your opponent has connected with a few punches or threatened you with a real submission, all you'll have to rely on is muscle memory and the comfort of those few basic moves you've managed to work deep into the knowledge of the flesh: the jab, the cross, the body kick, the clinch, maybe a takedown or two, the armbar and the guillotine choke. In the throes of first fear and exhaustion, all the fancy moves you covet disappear: the spinning back-fists and superman punches and *omoplata* shoulder locks. Strategy and thought go, too. The primordial instinct to brawl consumes you. Your chin flies up into danger and your punches lash out in whirlwinds; panic overcomes you when you're on the ground, drowning all the patience you've trained into yourself as a grappler. Or all that technique can't be translated into actual hostility and so dies where it sits: useless, like a paralyzed and peaceful appendage. A first fight is the domain of abandon and unconscious action, and only muscle memory will keep you alive.

The prefrontal cortex, compared with the more stripped-down, ancient amygdala, is painfully slow. Oftentimes, in the face of fear it won't even have time to get involved; by the time the rational part of the brain realizes what's happening, the amygdala has triggered automatic responses in the body and humans find themselves reacting "instinctively" rather than consciously. In order for the human body to respond in a more rational and concerted way to high-stress situations, like a fight, motor routines have to become ingrained through repetition, moves and techniques done over and over again, essentially rewiring the brain's response to specific kinds of fear. Repeated enough times, these skills become more ingrained in a region called the striatum, where the knowledge and ability become subconscious, and therefore much faster—a new instinctual. But if a skill is relatively new, the prefrontal cortex is still in charge of its execution, using its planning circuitry to walk the brain and the body through every step of a motion, which is a slow process, far too slow for the stresses of a fight.

Which is why soldiers and tightrope walkers and fighters train as much as they do, not just to learn techniques but to habituate themselves to the conditions of high-stress, high-fear situations so that their primal instincts to run or panic in the face of terror are overridden by new motor routines, drilled over time into unconsciousness, and those techniques can be utilized. Habit and repetition reduce terror through the simulation of terrifying conditions. If the brain and the body are exposed enough times to a specific fear without harm, the prefrontal cortex and the hippocampus (the part of the brain that stores memories and emotions) can override the amygdala and its primordial panic.

For attainment of self-knowledge, no Buddhist monastery or Parisian salon or school of psychological thought can compete with fighting. You can lie to a therapist; you can fake your way through meditation; you can obfuscate and color and cloud and satirize and demur and defer and calculate. You can convince yourself you're doing none of these things. But a first fight will show you yourself in all your flawed glory. This is what I learned that night in Manhattan. That sharp Michelle with the lightning-fast kicks is not a violent person; that slick David is full of testosterone and anger; that little Jon is burning with the desire to be a large man with enormous power in his hands, the power to harm. This is who they are and what was there for everyone to see that night. Whether what they discovered was good or bad is a matter for the moralists to debate, a social construct. But the purity of personality on display, the uncompromised humanity exposed, was an undeniable thing of beauty, beyond petty distinctions like good or bad. Those fighters stood on display in front of hundreds of people, stripped of clothing, excess weight, propriety, self-control, and all the other protective devices of the social contract, exposed for who they are. At its heart, fighting is a descent into atavism and a show of unfiltered identity, producing the kind of self-knowledge that comes in the panicked seconds before drowning. Technique is a fine thing, as are discipline and honor, but two minutes into a first fight, fueled by exhaustion and terror and the threat of humiliation, personality is everything.

If I'm right about this, that fighting shows us for who we really are, then what a bizarre thing for people to spend their lives running away from. What a thing to fear. Just think of the countless late nights spent drowning in religious longing or liquor or both, all the thousands of hours spent on analysts' couches, crying out for self-awareness, when all along it was available any night of the week at any bar in any American city for the price of a broken nose or a night in jail.

Which means that after forty long years of wondering and wandering, forty years spent searching for enlightenment and self-knowledge in books and sex and drugs and family and booze and therapy and philosophy and debate and dark nights of the soul and the life of the mind, I may finally find out who I am by simply walking into a cage. Am I a coward? A con man? A savage? A sadist? A technician? An artist? A brute? An intellectual? A sociopath? A humanitarian?

The answer will be written all over me as soon as the bell rings.

3

CRUEL YOUTH

(EIGHT MONTHS OUT)

The Fighter knew the crowd was always going to be on his opponent's side, a kid from some nothing east Texas town, barely in high school, fighting a full-grown man, so why not cultivate their animosity? Anything to shake off the nerves and get your name out there. But if the Fighter had any superstition or literature in him he would have realized that he was tempting the fighting gods and setting himself up for a fall by taunting a teenager. But he didn't, and even if he did, this was his first fight, too, and even though he was twenty years old, the Fighter was as nervous as the Kid was. When he got into the cage he had to do something to get rid of some of the steam and anxiety that had been building in him back in the dressing room. So he stomped his feet and shook his fist and threatened the Kid from across the cage and ran his thumb across his own throat in a slicing gesture, and the crowd booed him passionately. This was the loudest and most excited they had been all night, and the Fighter was enjoying playing the heel. It took him back to the days of watching professional wrestling with his father and brothers. This is how you get people's attention, he thought.

Thirty seconds later, after the Fighter, now buzzing on theatrical rage and the crowd's hostility, had come racing out of his corner and lunged with a reckless punch that missed the Kid by a foot, he began to realize what a mistake he'd made. A clinch sent them tumbling to the mat wrapped together, and the Fighter started to flail desperately. Fighting for him was about punching, not rolling around in another man's arms, and on the ground he was lost. The Kid, only sixteen but some kind of grappling prodigy and strangely calm for someone so young, threw his legs across the older man's chest and grabbed his wrist and wrenched it backward in a perfect armbar, pushing his hips up to put terrible pressure on the Fighter's elbow. An enormous roar came up from outside the cage. The Fighter had never felt such pain before or heard such a wild noise coming from a crowd. It whirled in his ears and made him dizzy. But even through the pain and the noise he could see that his attempts at intimidation had doomed him. After making a spectacle of himself by trying to scare a sixteen-year-old, he couldn't now just submit to him, even if submitting was the only reasonable thing to do. Not in front of all these people howling for his head. His pride would be shattered, and better a shattered arm than that. His sense of himself was tied up completely in being a fighter. So he held on hopelessly and resigned himself to his fate, even as his coaches and the crowd cried out for him to tap, and the Kid kept wrenching his arm back and a few people in the audience turned their faces away and the Fighter let out a horrible cry as his arm snapped at the elbow.

In a second the referee leapt in to stop the fight and the Kid bounded from his back to his feet with all the joy and exuberance of youth and victory, and the crowd was cheering madly for him, the loudest cheers of the night by far. While the Kid danced, the Fighter stood up and slumped back to his corner, cradling his now-useless arm with the other, and paced awkwardly, overcome with shame, hoping to be swallowed up by his cornermen and disappear.

The announcer, with his goatee and his long ponytail and his round tortoiseshell glasses (how out of place he seemed in a roomful of close-cropped Texas brutes), declared the Kid the winner and raised his arm, and the crowd went mad with cruel joy. The Fighter's mockeries had turned the Kid into the night's hero, and his loss had taken on metaphorical meaning. The announcer then asked the crowd to give the losing man a hand as well, for his courage. "He was too proud to tap, folks. He would rather get his arm broken than give up. Isn't he tough?" The crowd's applause was mild, however, and the Fighter could hear spectators in the front row, many of them fighters themselves, mocking him.

"Fool should have tapped."

"Why would you let your arm get broken like that?"

"That's not tough. That's ridiculous."

All the Fighter wanted now was to get back to the dressing room, to be out from under the oppressive gaze of all those judging eyes and out of earshot of the jokes. But this was just a minor-league event in a small Houston suburb, and there was no path set aside for the fighters to walk back to the dressing room, no money or space for that. So the young man and his trainers would have to work their way slowly through the crowd of spectators who were now clogging the aisles on their way to the bathroom or to buy a beer between fights. The Kid was wearing a cowboy hat now and whooping into the microphone and thanking Jesus and the audience was whooping back. Stuck in the crowd, the Fighter could feel their eyes on him. He hugged his broken arm tight and hoped no one would bump into him before he made it to a doctor. Following his coaches slowly through the crowd, he felt a familiar sadness wash over him.

Looking back now on that night in Houston seven years ago—a night when I'd driven 340 miles round-trip in a single day by myself just to attend some meaningless minor-league MMA event because I'd fallen hopelessly in love—with the benefit of experience and age and whatever wisdom comes from taking too many punches to the head, I believe I can see now much more clearly what the Fighter was aiming for than I could then.

At the time I assumed, like everyone else, that his attempts at intimidation were just a bit of theater and self-induced hypnosis, a way to get inside his opponent's head and calm his own nerves by riling himself up, a wail of misguided machismo that probably deserved to be mocked when it backfired so spectacularly. Now, though, I'm starting to think there was something more desperate and fatalistic going on in the fighter's mind, however subliminal, something darker and more primordial, some instinctual rage.

When he looked across the cage that night the Fighter, though just barely twenty years old himself, saw something awful standing before him. Not just a man looking to cause him physical harm, though that, too. No, what he saw that so terrified him and that made him lash out so absurdly was someone younger than he was, a vision of the future and a warning (maybe the young man's first) about the inexorable and unforgiving passing of time. Some ghost from his past. There, the young man may have heard over the shouts of the crowd, is the kid you once were; there is the youth you once had. Just like you, only stronger and better and faster and more devoted than you were then. At that moment maybe the Fighter realized that he wasn't just about to fight another person; he was about to take on the next generation, and his own obsolescence. Maybe for the first time in his life he felt his age. Perhaps he felt the first premonitory ache in his knees and the first shortness of breath. Maybe for the first time in his twenty carefree years, doubt crept into the Fighter's sense of himself as he stared at that reminder of fleeting youth now standing across the cage from him, mocking him with its perfect form and its unchallenged, unquestioned belief in that perfection. It's no surprise then that like an animal catching the shadow of a predator out of the corner of its eye, or like Lear, if Lear had been a twenty-year-old cage fighter rather than an old king on his heath, he panicked, flew into a rage, and shouted to the world his defiance and his refusal and his disdain. But in the end it all came out like fear, like terror from deep down in his soul, and ate him up.

In 1984 Larry Bird played Michael Jordan for the first time. At the time, Bird was twenty-seven years old and one of the undisputed kings of the National Basketball Association, and Jordan, just twenty-one, was the young phenomenon destined to usurp him. As a tune-up for the Olympic Games that summer a scrimmage had been arranged between a team made up of NBA stars, including Bird, and the men's national team, a team of amateurs led by Jordan, who had just finished his third, and last, year at the University of North Carolina. By that fall he would be in the NBA. Bird, like the Fighter in Houston, found himself unsure of what to do with his new unnameable fear of the future that Jordan embodied. He had always played basketball with the confidence that comes from youthful dominance, and the world splayed out before him. For the first time ever he felt rattled. So, during warm-ups, when Jordan's ball got away from him and came rolling over to the all-star team's side of the court, and Jordan, on the verge of superstardom and as full of confidence as any young man has ever been, came running over to retrieve it, Bird saw his opportunity to hold off, even if only for a few more seconds, the arrival of the force that would signal the beginning of his inevitable decline and irrelevance. So he picked up Jordan's ball, and as the younger man stood there politely waiting for it back, he hurled it violently over Jordan's head to the other end of the court, where it bounced into the long hallway leading to the locker room and disappeared. "Go get it," Bird told Jordan, turning away.

Andy and I are the same height and the same weight and we've been training for the same amount of time, so on paper any sparring session with him should be a fair one. But he's also half my age, which muddies the waters. Andy has broader shoulders than I do, more-defined arms, an overwhelming air of health and masculinity, a body in the throes of fitness and youth. Unfakeable, unmistakable, irreplaceable youth. "Silly, charming, beautiful youth," Joseph Conrad called it. He has something that I once had and can never have back. And when I had it I was too busy indulging my lowest desires to think about taking advantage of what my body was capable of when it was at its most capable—to even notice the youth I was squandering.

Andy and I start circling each other in the cage one evening in April, and I don't have a chance. He's faster than I am. With his young reflexes, he gets his punches off quicker. With those young eyes, he sees things I can't. And all the while he's telling me what I'm doing wrong—not cruelly, just casually and with the noblest intentions. He wants to help, which makes it so much worse: all that effortlessness and decency.

"You have to move your head," Andy says. *Yes, I know.* He jabs me twice in the face. "You have to move your feet." *Yes, I know.* He kicks me in the ribs. "Don't close your eyes." *Yes, yes, of course, I know.* I miss with a jab-cross combination and he quickly responds with one of his own. "Keep your hands up." *Right, got it, thank you, I know.* He hits me square on the nose, making my eyes water and scrambling my brain. "Fake feint move bob weave punch parry maintain your distance close the distance jab cross hook uppercut don't do that don't do that don't do that . . ."

Yes, I know!

I'm trying to be attentive and indignant and agitated and grateful all at the same time, but no human being can manage that, so my brain freezes up. I've become a punching bag. All the joy of fighting has drained out of me: the predictable, inevitable, humbling counterbalance to any previous warm delusions I've had about myself as a fighter.

Andy is having his way with me now—each punch landing on my nose or my chin, each kick crashing into my thigh or my side, making my head pound and my ribs ache—and I've lost my sense of intention. Aesthetics and effectiveness have gone out the window, leaving me with desperation, which is not something to base a strategy on. I'm just moving around the ring for movement's sake, to prove that I'm there and alive and capable of something, *anything!*—a refusal to go quietly, a protest against decline and incapacity and age and death. Sparring has ceased to be a training tool and become instead an exercise in existential declaration, a yawp in the night.

I may be just a perpetual amateur fighter with no aspirations beyond the desire to fight just one fight before I drift off into middle age and decline, and yet nothing in my life makes me quite as upset as an unsuccessful day of sparring—not an argument with my wife, not a lapse in my writing career, not a rightward shift in the country's political affinities. It doesn't matter that I have no future as a fighter. It doesn't matter that I started too late in life.

It doesn't matter that I was never a great athlete to begin with. It doesn't even matter that I may not actually *be* a fighter, in the metaphysical sense of the word—a fighter *in my essence*.

This is the hardest thing about sparring: After a good round you feel like a king; after a bad one you feel like anyone you pass on the street could knock you out. And whatever emotional state you were in when you left the gym you'll remain in until you walk back into the gym. I hold on to my sparring successes like family heirlooms and my failures like the symptoms of a lingering illness. This is why long weekends and vacations are dangerous. A bad sparring match can ruin a two-week trip if you're not careful. It messes with your sense of self, of personal value, of presence; it jolts your emotional equilibrium. Perhaps more than anyone—more than concert pianists, more than surgeons, more than quarterbacks—a fighter's confidence, illusory or not, is everything.

And what does it mean, anyway, being a fighter? One of my coaches, Elijah, once told me that what makes a fighter is the instinct to smell blood and attack, to sense an opponent's injury and exploit it. Well, I'm not sure I have that kind of callous monomania in me. I sometimes forget, in the thrill of sparring, in the exhaustion of training, in the narcissistic exhilaration of postfight-preshower mirror-gazing, that fighting requires cruelty and inhumanity.

This is a true story: Whenever I imagine my upcoming fight, I picture my coaches screaming at me to keep kicking a leg my opponent has started favoring, and I can't do it. The crowd is howling and flailing like animals, crying out for me to kick that leg, kick that leg, *kick that leg!* And I can't do it. My opponent is limping around, unable to defend himself, just sitting out there like a big target, waiting for me to finish the fight by kicking his leg, and *I cannot do it.* And then something remarkable happens. All of a sudden the ring is bathed in a warm light and I'm floating serenely two feet off the canvas on a cloud of infinite calm, mercy, and self-awareness. I step away from my opponent and signal the audience to quiet down (which they do, in my imagination), then I turn toward the referee and I say something like "He's had enough. I will fight him no more." Like Chief Joseph now; this is my *noble moment*. And I sit down on my stool in my corner and take off my gloves and smile beatifically, knowing that my 0–1 record (TKO: Retirement, due to an excess of moral zeal and a sudden recognition of the metaphysical interconnectedness of all human souls) will live forever with an asterisk beside it placed there by humanity itself, like a medal hung around the neck of a Nobel Peace Prize winner, sending a message to future generations: here was one who sacrificed glory for mercy. I will become legendary for my decency and my forbearance. People will write about me and the night I chose humanity over victory.

This is how I dream about my first, and likely only, fight. *This* is my fantasy.

Testosterone levels peak in men in their late teens and early twenties. When men reach thirty, their testosterone levels start declining by about 1 percent per year, resulting in a drop in aggression and a decrease in both muscle mass and muscle strength. Since more fast-twitch muscle fibers are lost than slow-twitch fibers, the remaining muscles don't react as quickly as they once did.

The part of the brain in charge of motor control starts to decline at forty. Neural cells rely on well-insulated nerve fibers to smoothly and quickly send commands to muscles. This insulation, a sheet of fat called myelin, builds up in the nerve fibers during adolescence, but production starts to slow down around

forty, slowing electrical conduction and therefore communica-
tion between the body and the brain. The lower the frequency of
these electrical signals over time, the slower the resulting physical movement, whether catching a ball or throwing a punch.

The body produces less melatonin the older you get. By the
time you're forty, you're sleeping two fewer hours a night on aver-
age than you were when you were eighteen. Just when I need my
sleep the most, when my body is getting bruised and beaten and
wrenched in preparation for a fight against a man half my age (a
man flush with melatonin) and is most in need of restoration,
sleep is beginning to abandon me.

My lung capacity has been slowly sinking for twenty years
(aided, no doubt, by fifteen years of smoking: a young man's pre-
emptive attack on his future self), my body is losing more bone
every year than it's producing, and my grip strength is declining,
which will make it harder for me to grab my opponent's neck
and arms and legs as we scramble for position against the cage
and wrestle for control on the ground and tie up during boxing
exchanges and generally try to tear each other apart.

In your late thirties you begin to lose muscle mass and function, resulting in less strength and mobility. Researchers believe
one cause of age-related sarcopenia (from the Greek for "lack
of flesh") is the reduction in the number of brain cells sending
electrical signals to muscles.

There is some evidence that myelin starts to fray a decade
later in the regions of the brain responsible for cognitive functions than it does in its motor-control areas. Which means my
brain can fully understand how poorly it's starting to communicate with my body and the depths of my physical collapse.
There's something cruel about this quirk of biology: to be able to
comprehend with perfect mental clarity your physical and mental decline but not be able to stop it. It's like some ancient curse

from a Greek myth, like a poetic and ironic punishment from the gods.

So, doctor, what's the diagnosis?

Just this: That you've chosen to fight your first and only fight at the exact moment your body is beginning its irresistible descent into incapacity.

Very wise.

A few days after my sparring session with Andy, I arrive at the gym to find a small herd of sixteen-year-old blond boys I've never seen before milling about before class. They're new students who've decided to welcome the spring by learning to fight, each bumbling and clumsy and shy and entirely without skill or conviction but brimming with life and optimism, clear eyed and full of hope. This is typical. Kids like these seem to appear from out of nowhere every spring around the gym, like flowers after a long winter, each fresh and awkward and timid. And so impossibly blond. They look like schoolyard extras from a 1950s sitcom or, in my darker moments, poster children for the Hitler Youth. Doing a bit of quick math, I realize it would take exactly two and a half of them to equal my age, so of course I immediately hate them all.

As I wait for class to begin, I start to devise a strategy for dealing with these wide-eyed reminders of my mortality. I'm torn between two warring instincts: the avuncular and the selfish. I can't decide between passing on the knowledge I've gained and keeping them drowning in the dark for as long as I can. Should I be decent and extend a welcoming hand and show them the ropes, play the role of the gracious, patient older man at the gym with wisdom to share to willing ears? I think I could enjoy being the sage for whom communal evolution is more important than individual gain. Yes, I could play noble.

Or should I, like Larry Bird staring down Michael Jordan, aim to hobble them while I still have the chance, before they learn how to fight back, torment them with my knowledge without ever offering it to them, hiding my resentment and fear of obsolescence behind a mask of tough love? Should I do them in before they cut me down?

Choosing a strategy for dealing with the youth of the world will have to wait. It's too much to think about at noon on a Tuesday, and besides, I know that how I treat a sixteen-year-old novice fighter on any given day will depend on my mood. So I just pick one of them to partner with and we begin to move around and throw light jabs at each other. The experience immediately reminds me of every round of sparring I've ever gone through with every boy under twenty. They're clumsy and awkward but so full of youth and spastic energy, so full of desperate ardor, like a Romantic poet with a premonition he won't live to see thirty—candles who find beauty even in being snuffed out. Their light punches either come at me in perfect, predictable straight lines like tiny machines or flail wildly from bizarre angles. I can see their kicks coming from a mile off. There's no smoothness to their movements and hardly any danger in their attacks. But I can't match them for speed or enthusiasm when we're scrambling for control of each other's bodies on the ground, reaching wildly for legs and hips and necks to gain leverage, so I have to use calm and conservation and guile.

I also have to be patient in those rare moments when they catch me in a bad position or hit me in the nose, rather than panic and equate every mistake with a tragedy. This is what's known as the wisdom of age: having lived through a million beatings and knowing none of them is permanent. A young person, blinded by solipsism and lust, thinks each moment is the last moment he'll ever know, that it's the end of the world, and so they treat every move they make as a life-and-death affair. But the older person has perspective and knows the world never ends and that you'll be punished for whatever decision you make. A great calm starts to settle in the mind of the fighter once he's learned that there's no logic or meaning to the universe. Meaning muddles fighting. Resignation clarifies it.

This is the kind of wisdom I use against my young opponents to offset their physical gifts and boundless vitality. My tactics aren't just psychological—they're existential. This is an important strategy to develop, just as important as my technical skill and cardiovascular endurance, because the person I'll be fighting just eight months from now will most likely be closer in age and spirit to these young men than to me, and if I hope to beat him I'll have to approach him philosophically and not rely on any physical advantages. As a perpetual amateur staring down middle age with aching hips, I must find hope in hopelessness and strategy in existential dread, or at least cosmic resignation.

And so every sparring session becomes a battle between life experience and unbridled youth. These young men leap all over me, springing back and forth and this way and that way, clawing at me and grabbing on desperately and heaving great breaths and using all their strength on every takedown and every punch as if it were their last, inadvertently scraping me with their fingernails and kneeing me in the crotch and elbowing me in the face in their mad scrambles for dominance. Their energy and abandon are too much for me to keep up with. I lose every time I try to play their way. But I win when I'm patient and conserve my energy and affect an air of indifference and wait for them to grow impatient, and by doing this I slowly suck all the passion and enthusiasm and lust for fighting, and for life, right out of them. They throw five, ten, even twenty wild punches in a row, but I play defensive, and the blows all bounce meaninglessly off my forearms and slide off my shoulders. I want them to feel not just the weight of my body on theirs and the frustration of incapacity but the weight of life and the frustration of accumulated disappointment. I want them to know, for those five or ten minutes, what I've learned in forty years: that life is about the slow but inevitable triumph of gravity and the irresistible grinding of the mill. I want to give my young opponents just a glimpse of this reality, of the blinding belittling indifference of the universe. I want to *exhaust* them, to hold their generation off, to fight for my claim on the world they want to take from me. Which, when I think about it, seems like a cruel thing to do to a teenager just trying out a new hobby. But whether these kids know it or not, there are bigger issues at stake here, and I've got my soul to think about.

The Greek lyric poet Pindar composed numerous odes to champions of the ancient Olympic Games—wrestlers, boxers, sprinters, chariot racers, mule racers, even pipe players. These poems extolled all the manly virtues considered fundamental to the spirit of the ancient Greeks: glory, courage, endurance, strength, and, most important, youth.

By the time of the 446 BCE Games, however, Pindar was a seventy-seven-year-old man contemplating the end of his life. Composing the last of his victory odes, to the wrestler Aristomenes of Aegina, Pindar showed himself for the first time less concerned with the splendor of physical genius than the transitory nature of life and joy. He no longer saw the delight in youth he used to. Instead he saw it as the greatest of all human delusions and the cruelest of life's tragedies.

> In a little moment groweth up the delight of men;
> yea and in like sort falleth it to the ground
> when a doom adverse hath shaken it.

> Things of a day—what are we, and what not?
> Man is a dream of shadows.

So, what do I have to rely on that a kid doesn't have? I have cunning and guile and wit and resignation and patience and deception and stubbornness and cruelty and numbness and a more nuanced relationship with morality and the conventions of fair play: a whole lifetime's worth of accumulated knowledge and wisdom that transcends the provincial world of fighting and that has a sense of perspective and metaphor to it. I also have a stronger instinct toward self-preservation than I did when I was young, which means I won't go diving recklessly into a fight. A young man, flush with a sense of immortality and bubbling over with testosterone, will unwisely throw caution to the wind and run chin first into punching exchanges or carelessly leave an arm out in the world to get caught and twisted in the thrill of the moment. But I'm building a fighting strategy around my devotion to life, my awareness of its fragility, my jealousy over its continuation, and my fear of its ending.

It's common for fighters to talk about being willing to die when they get in a ring or a cage, but it's a young person's luxury to claim indifference to death. A forty-year-old knows it's ridiculous to be willing to die for something as inconsequential as a fight, especially when you're sixteen and there are so many other inconsequential things left to be done. And no matter what fighters and coaches like to say, indifference to mortality is not just ridiculous from a biological perspective; it's strategically counterproductive. My dread and desire for self-preservation, rather than being a hindrance to my success as a fighter, have become the centerpiece of my fighting strategy. Norman Mailer once wrote that part of Muhammad Ali's genius as a boxer lay in his "fidelity to his mood." Well, I fight out of fidelity to a whole overarching philosophy of life-preservation, which makes me cautious and careful and crafty. Diving into a life-threatening situation with abandon may be a great way to feel alive, and it may even provide a temporary tactical advantage against an overwhelmed opponent, but being strategically covetous of health is the way to show true devotion to life, and to win in the end. This means concentrating on defense, learning how to escape chokes and slip punches, to avoid unnecessary damage and spot tiny opportunities. It means staying out of wild, hurling punching exchanges that exist only for the sake of proving toughness to oneself and others, even at the expense of one's tender brain and body. A privilege of age is caring less about what others think about you than when you were young, and there's strategic advantage in that. Insecurities can be preyed on. So I'll let *that* be my genius, and hopefully triumph not in spite of my age but because of it.

I imagine I'll keep training this way until that day comes when some eighteen-year-old with his flawless body and sponge-like mind and blinding speed and lack of age-borne existential dread does me in at last, when the cleverness of my cognitive mind can no longer hold off the collapse of my motor control and my body finally gives in to fate. And when that dark day comes, I hope I'll find some solace in knowing that the cycle will go on repeating and repeating forever—that one day, without fail, some new kid, even younger and stronger and faster and more perfect than the one who made me obsolete, will knock at my conqueror's door to show him his future, to make him confront his mortality and mock his biological collapse and break his spirit. Even amid all that youthful athletic splendor and strength, a warning is always lingering in the back of every human mind, even those too young and beautiful to hear it, getting louder as the days go by: this too shall pass. Or better, *moriemur*: we shall all die.

4

THE WEIGHT OF HISTORY

(SEVEN MONTHS OUT)

There was a time when Gleason's boxing gym, with its peeling paint, aging equipment, and air-conditioning-free squalor, fit perfectly in this neighborhood in western Brooklyn, which for decades was trapped in a slow implosion, each year more dilapidated and violent than the last. Now, surrounded by coffee shops and boutique clothing stores and multimillion-dollar condominiums and all the other trappings of gentrification, the gym feels like a museum exhibit, like a relic from an earlier, more sordid New York. And climbing the long, narrow staircase and passing through the affectless metal door into that steaming warehouse and walking between all those ancient rings with their torn canvases and the small weightlifting area with its ancient barbells and fraying medicine balls and looking around at all those fighters who are pulled apart when they clinch rather than taught how to fight there, fighters who never use their feet or their knees to attack, fighters who would be lost on the ground and so never go there—one can't help but feel like it's a cathedral for a sport from another time as well. A time when a pair of fists was enough to win a fight.

I sought out Gleason's because I wanted to learn the secrets of this older world: the subtle fakes and feints and weaves and parries, the crafty footwork that can propel a fighter in and out of an opponent's range with minimal movement, the pivots and bumps and shuffles that conspire to flummox before punches even start getting thrown: the art of movement and misdirection. MMA may be the new world of fighting, but these ancient arts, I decided, would be my defense against the kicks and submissions and overwhelming urgency of the next generation.

Such is the liberating genius of mixed martial arts: that fighters can create their own particular language by choosing the traditions that best amplify their strengths and disguise their weaknesses. No two are the same. A man who spent his high school years wrestling will likely make that the foundation for his style inside the cage, repeatedly dropping his opponents to the ground and smothering them, while a woman who finds herself with a natural affinity for Muay Thai may use the long push kicks of that tradition to keep opponents at a distance. And so a fighter like me, whose body and soul aren't inclined toward grappling, can devote himself to his boxing, build a vocabulary from there, and hope it suffices.

From his favorite spot inside Gleason's, next to a beat-up metal cabinet bursting at the hinges with old gloves and pads, my boxing coach, Dorrius Forde, preaches to me his life's philosophy. Defense and evasiveness, he tells me, are the keys to the mysteries of the sweet science. There wisdom lies. And so, like a devotee eager for religious understanding, every day I practice the ancient art, bobbing and weaving by ducking repeatedly under a frayed rope hanging between two columns covered in peeling paint in the center of the gym, sliding my feet forward and backward, while Dorrius watches, skeptical of my devotion. "Move your head! Bend at the waist!" he yells at me over and over again, to little avail. This is due partly to exhaustion but also to the instinct for self-preservation. Bobbing and weaving are skills I long to acquire but can't afford to master: lean too low as a mixed martial artist and you'll get a shin or a knee to the face.

Dorrius then takes me inside the ring, where he repeatedly prods me with long swimming noodles to drive his philosophy home, calling out his commands—duck, slip, pull back, circle out!—in a thick Caribbean accent I secretly blame whenever I duck when I should have pulled back or circle out instead of slipping and take a chunk of Styrofoam to the face as a result. He makes me shadowbox for rounds and rounds and run for endless minutes on the treadmill and the StairMaster, and stands over me as I do countless crunches and push-ups, since endurance and physical implacability are good substitutes for youth as well. He arranges sparring sessions for me with fighters of all different sizes and strengths and speeds to make sure my defense can stand up to all the varieties of offense: the long and lanky attack, the overwhelming violence of a charging bull, the elegant counterpuncher.

All of Dorrius's students are, in their own ways, a reflection of his philosophy of elusion. And so everyone I spar with at Gleason's is nearly impossible to lay a glove on. Seven, ten, even fifteen rounds will go by over the course of a two-hour session on a Sunday morning ("This is my church," Dorrius says proudly of these Sabbath sparring klatches), and I spend nearly all of them chasing my opponents around, trying to pin them in corners so I can land at least one clean blow per round. But each one of them has paid attention to the wisdom of their teacher and learned the art of tucking their chin behind their gloves and leaning back just slightly out of punching range and putting their hips on a swivel, of shifting their feet just slightly to take themselves out of harm's way, of parrying my punches with their gloves while shifting their heads just off the center line and bobbing and weaving underneath my hooks and deflecting my crosses off their shoulders. Not quite the seasoned Dorrius acolyte the others are yet, and bursting with lust and passion as I get closer to my fight, I leave my own head unmoving and available too often and get counterpunched for my ignorance and obstinacy.

Dorrius is fifty-three now, but in his youth he was a boxer with promise in his native Guyana. But prizefighting is no way to make a living, and for a short time in the early nineties, with young children at home and his career as a fighter stalling, Dorrius took a job as a sparring partner for the legendary Puerto Rican fighter Hector "Macho" Camacho. At the time Camacho was one of the best boxers in the world, a champion in three weight classes, and being his sparring partner was dangerous work. Dorrius and his fellow sparring partners (each of whom took home a few hundred dollars a week for the eight-week training camp) took to calling their daily sessions with Camacho "the blood bank," and more than one got hurt badly by the champion.

"Surviving as a sparring partner is no easy way of life," Dorrius tells me one afternoon. "I told myself when I was there, 'You have to find a way not to get beat up every day.' That's when I really started developing as a defensive fighter. I realized I had to be slick and evasive because I had to survive." Out of such circumstances are philosophies born.

———

Dorrius is right, of course. Boxing is the art of movement, and there's no heroism in a concussion or chronic traumatic encephalopathy, the degenerative brain disease caused by repetitive trauma that's the curse of prizefighters and football players—no glory in memory loss or depression or progressive dementia. After a lifetime of boxing, Dorrius still speaks with a clear tongue and thinks with a subtle mind, while many of his former opponents and sparring partners and friends are slow or muddled or mangled or even dead.

But Dorrius is wrong at the same time. I want to learn to move with the subtlety of the dancer as much as anyone, but it would be a lie if I said I don't want to get hit as well. If health and survival were all I were concerned with, I wouldn't be sparring for two hours every Sunday morning. I wouldn't have signed up for an MMA fight. I wouldn't be in the gym at all. No, there is something larger at work in me than the desire for artistic and athletic competence and self-preservation, something visceral and primordial. Something self-*destructive* I'm searching for. I've avoided physical confrontation my entire life. I mastered evasion long, long ago.

Sometimes when I think about my fight I wonder if I would prefer to win a bloodless artful decision or lose a giant, bloody, bruising, horrifying war, one spectators couldn't watch but couldn't turn away from, either—the kind of fight people still speak about years later. I think the latter would suit me better. One would tell me that I learned something, but the other would tell me that I *lived* through something. A loss, especially a dramatic loss, would be more relevant to my existential concerns, as well. It would tell me at last that I can handle getting beaten up after all those years of terror at the prospect. I haven't been plagued by a lifelong desire to win a fight, only the desire not to cower from one.

I think I might even like to get knocked out, just to see what it feels like. Former heavyweight boxing champion James J. Braddock said getting knocked out by Joe Louis felt like getting smashed in the face with a lightbulb. "I thought half my head was blowed off," he said. That sounds like something. To be knocked unconscious by another person would be a truly immersive experience, an undeniable, complete experience. "Since feeling is first / who pays any attention / to the syntax of things / will never wholly kiss you," e. e. cummings wrote. I've had too much syntax in my life, too many words and explanations. My brain is sick with it. I want to live wholly, free once and for all from the mitigating forces of grammar, words, technical proficiency, and self-preservation.

Sometimes, when the mood strikes him, I get to spar with Dorrius. These are always the greatest days at the gym, days when my education comes in great torrents rather than fits and starts, when I get to experience, even if just for a moment and at my physical and emotional expense, something like greatness and artistry. Surely no pedagogical method in the world is more effective or more intimate than repeated, unblocked blows to the head of a willing student. The lessons are literally pounded in.

Even at fifty-three, with a large round belly poking out over his groin guard, Dorrius is beautiful to watch. His jabs flash at my head from out of nowhere, always finding their way past my raised guard to my chin. His feet are always moving, subtly shifting this way and that to insinuate himself into his punching range and then out of mine, leaving me punching at air. Despite being out of shape, he's never winded, because he barely has to move at all. I'm usually too worried about his hands to notice his feet, but when he spars with others they're all I watch, trying to unravel their mysteries: I sense that the secret to success in boxing can be found in those subtle shifts and pivots. Sometimes Dorrius won't throw a single punch during a round, just move his head, slipping and bobbing, so that all my punches miss. And this, Dorrius tells me after the round is over and I'm doubled over in the corner, is the most important lesson in boxing: anyone coming in off the street can punch; what makes a fighter is knowing how to *avoid* getting punched. In this way Dorrius Forde distinguishes between the poets and the brutes of the world.

When you begin sparring with real fighters, you learn quickly that nearly all of your strikes will miss and that the strikes they throw at you will come so fast and cloaked in so much misdirection that you won't have the time or the presence of mind to defend against them, no matter how trained you may think you are. A great striker, like a great chess player, will use one strike to set up another, will bait his opponent with a jab to make him drop his hands or shift his weight just enough to make him vulnerable to a cross or a head kick. A strike rarely exists on its own, and the key to a successful combination is disguising which punch or kick is the centerpiece until it's too late to do anything about it. Before you know what's happening you're trapped in a whirlwind of punches and kicks and knees and elbows, entirely at someone else's mercy.

Sometimes Dorrius will throw three or four jabs so fast to my chin that I'll find myself thinking about how I should be defending myself but be unable to do so. *Bang bang bang bang!*—all in a row, and I'm standing there pleading with myself, "Close your guard, block the punch, what are you waiting for?" but they're simply too fast. One fake will freeze me and three real

punches will follow in a burst while I stand there in quickly drying concrete. I know that I should be parrying the punch, using
my glove to slide it off the line to my face, or covering up entirely
to take the force of the blows on my forearm, but that kind of
speed coupled with that kind of pain scrambles the brain. The
message gets muddled before it can get to my body. The sensation of powerlessness in these situations is overwhelming, almost metaphysical, like drowning in an ocean at night or getting
marooned on a desert island: it puts you in mind of your insignificance and the vastness of the natural world. *Alone, alone, all,
all alone / Alone on a wide wide sea! / And never a saint took pity
on / My soul in agony*. Often I'm so mesmerized by how quickly
these strikes come that a kind of paralysis takes me over, like I'm
immobilized by aesthetic admiration.

In the hands of a master, strikes take on different textures
and tones, like a painter throwing a splash of umber into a smear
of red to give it subtler meaning. A jab, for example, can be used
as a tool to measure distance, brushing your chin without any ill
intent, lulling you into a state of deluded confidence even as it
sets you up for another, more forceful shot. Or it can flash out at
your nose quickly, with a whipping strike, to disorient you and
fill you with petulance and rage, preying on your pride and van-
ity. It can come straight through or arch over your outstretched
hands or leap in from below, where you won't see it coming. It
can hook in past your peripheral vision and land behind your
ear, disturbing the delicate balance of your vestibular system, or
come in a straight line directly at your chin. It can be thrown
at your stomach, knocking the wind out of you, or hard at your
face to stun you. It can fake and feint and throw off your timing
and make you doubt yourself. Masters of the jab use it to poke
and tap and madden and intimidate and explore and sting and
annoy and open up opportunities for other, stronger punches.

Sometimes Dorrius will just hold his jabbing hand straight out at my nose through a whole round, like a spear, and barely even touch me with it, just block my vision and push me back. He says he learned this technique in Cuba.

But it's only when you're in the cage with a great fighter that you really appreciate the art. You can watch a fight and admire its beauty, even be moved by it, but this is only the passive appreciation of the observer, like listening to a piece of music or staring at a canvas. To actually fight an artist is to experience beauty in your bones and your flesh and in the adrenaline shooting through your nerves. To *feel* sublimity. Poets and novelists would sacrifice every earthly delight to be able to get that deep into the blood of their audiences.

Albert Camus was an amateur boxer. Ezra Pound sparred with Ernest Hemingway in his apartment in Paris. Norman Mailer used to train with light heavyweight champion José Torres. Even Lord Byron studied boxing with John Jackson, a former champion of England whom the poet nicknamed the "Emperor of Pugilism." There's a natural creative affinity that exists between writing and fighting because they're both alchemical arts—the greatest writers take unmanageable life and press it into something meaningful, and the best fighters convert their basest and most violent instincts into something beautiful. "The purpose of literature," T. S. Eliot wrote, "is to turn blood into ink."

Writers also recognize that a fighter—despite all the trainers and cornermen and referees and fans, despite even his opponent—is out there on his own, squaring off with himself every time. "A boxer, like a writer, must stand alone," wrote A. J. Liebling. I think that's probably true. Then again, maybe, like so many writers who cover fighters, Liebling really just wanted to believe that there's a connection between what he does and what they do, so he came up with an epigram to make it so. In this regard, writers have got it all over fighters: we get to create the world they only live in.

Or maybe it's just that all that time we writers spend locked in our heads makes our bodies cry out for action, action, *action!* For some of us, fighting isn't a risk; it's a refuge from the loud-mouthed battle that constantly rages in our brains, all those opinions and critiques and internal sparring matches—*put this word here, no, switch it back!* Fighting offers freedom from the tyranny of the mind.

One day Dorrius shares with me the secrets of the double-jab-cross, one of boxing's most potent combinations, where a fighter distracts his opponent with two quick left hands, moving his feet forward and his body into range "behind the jab," and then comes over their glove with a strong right hand. Something about the craftiness and simplicity of the 1–1–2 combination speaks to me. I decide to make it the centerpiece of my strategy, something elemental to rely on when the Great Fear sets in. Dorrius also puts a mantra in my head to rely on during my fight, a phrase to remind myself that fighting isn't about the single heroic knock-out punch but the slow exploratory work done by a prodding jab over time to artfully draw out an opponent and lull him and expose him. The jab doesn't even have to cause any damage, Dorrius tells me: *Just touch him. Just touch him.*

Growing up poor in Guyana in the 1960s, Dorrius dreamed of becoming a professional boxer and escaping his third-world paralysis. Two of his uncles were fighters—one boxed in the 1972

Olympics, the other fought for the world featherweight championship twice—and they began to train their nephew when he was only seven. By the time he was fifteen, Dorrius was competing as an amateur, and three years after that he turned professional. Once, he says, at a tournament in Guyana, he upset the Cuban champion and became a national hero. Though the fight was only broadcast on the radio, Dorrius tells me he was recognized wherever he went. "I became a household name," he says. "All the kids knew me. I was the Mike Tyson of Guyana. They *still* talk about that fight."

Boxing is full of these kinds of legends. The air inside an old gym is heavy with them. They're in the walls and the mats, wet from decades of sweat. Mythmaking and tradition are as much a part of boxing as the fighting itself. Take the poster hanging on the wall at Gleason's next to the speed bags advertising an upcoming fight at the Five Star Banquet Hall in Queens. In big, bold, fiery letters the poster touts a young boxer named Ariel "El Kuman" Lopez as the "New Mexican Sensation." Just below these letters, in a far smaller and more modest font, is Lopez's record: 1–0–0. Ariel Lopez has only fought one fight. One *sensational* fight, no doubt. Nobody understands the value of a good story better than a fight promoter.

In MMA gyms people talk about moves they learned the night before and fights they watched last weekend. In boxing gyms the old trainers, with their expanding bellies and receding hairlines and booming voices and endless games of gin, talk about fights they saw years ago and victories they earned decades before and fighters long dead. Some of the stories are true, others amplified, if not made up entirely. There is as much lore and tradition and mythmaking in a boxing gym as there is in a Catholic church. And just like in a Catholic church, on the walls hang pictures of the saints, the heroes of all those myths—Joe Louis and Muhammad Ali and Sonny Liston—placed there to inspire, yes, but whose presence can suffocate as well. Looking at them, you can feel the weight of all that tradition and mythology and righteousness pressing down on you, running backward through eternity from Mayweather to Tyson to Hagler to Marciano to Dempsey to Johnson to the British bare-knucklers, who would fight for fifty rounds or more, all the way back to the boxers of ancient Rome, who would often fight to the death. A banner with a quote from Virgil's *Aeneid*, written during the Imperial Roman period, covers one of the walls at Gleason's, daring you but also putting your achievements and your life in perspective: "Now, whoever has courage, and a strong and collected spirit in his breast, let him come forward, lace on the gloves and put up his hands." Boxing has been around forever. It's old and settled, and it's sick with tradition and history. It's there in the long, hot stairwell and the heaving, stinking locker room. It's there in the ring. It's there in that two-thousand-year-old epigram hanging over your head. Boxing is beautiful and poetic and scientific, but like all history it will smother you to death if you're not careful.

Maybe this is why MMA captivated me in a way boxing never did. Searching for the most effective way to fight, mixed martial artists in the 1990s did away with all the cultural traditions that had been handed down from generation to generation, from master to student, all those forms and costumes and rituals and rules, all that religious meaning and all those connections to the mystical world, to the metaphysical realm, all the suffocating ghosts and smothering spirits and ancestors and superstitions of the old world. When I started fighting I was looking for liberation: from my history, from my expectations, from everything I'd built for myself over the previous thirty-three years. So I wasn't about to take on the weight of some other history in the process. MMA is too young to be burdened by tradition and the nightmare of history. Its very nature is liberation.

An essential part of the story American Jews have been telling for the past hundred years is that we're a peace-loving people, floating high above the malice and rage of our gentile tormentors. This idealization of purity and passivity is a way to distinguish ourselves from the "other," with its irrational hatreds and unimaginable violence. In fact, the whole reason we're in America is because we spent so many cruel centuries in Europe and the Middle East. So, growing up, I took it for granted that my family line was simply one long, unbroken, and unblemished thread of nonviolence leading back to Brooklyn and Chicago and Russia and Poland, all the way to the Garden of Eden. Nothing my father or grandfathers said or did gave me any reason to believe otherwise. Fighting was for *them*, not us. I don't recall hearing a single story about any fighting ancestors.

But recently I was given an old black-and-white photo of a Jewish boxer named Alex that suggests a different history. In the photo, Alex, my first cousin thrice removed (the words "My loving cousin Alex" were written along the top border by my great-grandmother Esther Kornbluth), is wearing nothing but a pair of short dark shorts, posing in the traditional boxer's stance: one foot bladed behind the other, his jabbing fist way out in front, the other placed just below the chin. Alex looks like a bantamweight, maybe even smaller. He's skinny and lacking in muscle definition, but he has sizable fists and a great big Semitic nose and a great big bush of thick curly black hair on his head and a great big smile on his face. He doesn't look like he's capable of hurting a thing, yet there he is, a boxer. Was there something in Alex that passed

through the Kornbluth bloodline to me, skipping two generations as it went, a fighter's recessive gene, perhaps?

The picture of Alex was taken in the 1930s, at the height
of Jewish pugilistic achievement. Boxing was full of Jews back
in the early part of the twentieth century, as common as Irish-
men and Italians and African Americans. Fighters like Benny
"The Ghetto Wizard" Leonard, the lightweight champion of
the world, who fought more than two hundred fights, winning
almost all of them, but who died after suffering a heart attack
in the ring at the age of fifty-one while plying his new trade as a
referee. And Barney Ross (born Dov-Ber David Rosofsky), who
dreamed of being a Talmudic scholar but who lost his faith and
turned to a life of crime and boxing after his father was killed in
a robbery at the family grocery story in a Chicago slum. And Al
"Bummy" Davis, who fought with a Jewish star embroidered on
his shorts, and who was killed at the age of twenty-five, in the
prime of his fighting career, after thwarting an armed robbery at
a bar in a Brooklyn neighborhood run by Murder Incorporated,
which carried out contract killings for the mob. Bummy was shot
three times inside the bar but only succumbed after chasing the
thieves into the street, where he took the fourth and fatal bullet.
Battling Levinsky. Kid Kaplan. Herbie Kronowitz. Mushy Cal-
lahan. Abe Attell, "The Little Hebrew." "Chrysanthemum Joe"
Choynski. Slapsie Rosenbloom. Abe "The Newsboy" Holland-
ersky. Joe Glick. There's a lineage worthy of the House of David.

These men, like so many boxers, rose out of squalor and poverty and the great American ethnic hazing of the late nineteenth
and early twentieth centuries. They came from the backwater
ghetto of Bushwick in Brooklyn (where my grandmother was
born and raised) and the pushcart crowds of Chicago's Maxwell
Street and the impoverished insanity of Manhattan's Lower East
Side, where every five years a new ethnic group seemed to appear

from off one of the nearby docks, all their belongings crammed into a single suitcase, after escaping some wretchedness and deprivation across the Atlantic, to vie with whatever ethnic groups had come before them fleeing their own wretchedness for a slice of the great American pie—Jewish kids and Italian kids and Irish kids and German kids, all at war in the streets of Manhattan. It's one of the oldest and most abiding traditions our country has, as much a part of the American myth as the Old West and the beach at Normandy: boxing as a way out from under the great weight of history and poverty.

But after World War II, Jews began to gain social acceptance and economic mobility and political influence, and as they integrated and ingratiated themselves into America and moved out of the ghettos and into the suburbs, they realized that the need to climb into a ring and take hundreds of blows to the head for a living had disappeared. In a burst of mass social evolution, the sons and daughters of Abraham and the shtetls moved on to other, less suicidal, professions, and Jewish fighters, who had been all over the boxing world for the first thirty years of the twentieth century, vanished from the ring. It wasn't long before no one could imagine Jews fighting, not even Jews.

And I'm the child of those Jews, the realization of all their peace-filled suburban dreams, nurtured in crowded tenement buildings and sweltering tanneries and blood-splattered boxing rings: *someday we'll get out.* I'm living the American dream they bled for; I'm the embodiment of their most fantastical hopes: a Jew finally free of all of history's bottomless malice. Yet there's something missing from my perfect life, this very sweet, safe, suburban life my ancestors dreamed of, some emptiness of experience, some desire for authenticity that seems to find satisfaction only in fighting and other acts of indecency and risk. It's this desire, I think, that drives the Jews of my generation back into Bushwick and the Lower East Side, to the bewilderment of our grandparents, who fought so hard to get out, who longed for a land of tree-lined streets and manicured lawns, for whom trees and lawns may as well have been lining the streets of heaven itself. Growing up, I couldn't bring myself to believe that the soulless world of shopping malls and parking lots I was being raised in was the American Dream my ancestors had longed for. Where they saw a haven and a harbor, a place safe and secure and quiet and civilized and free of all those urban threats that had tormented them for so many generations, free of hysterical anti-Semitic mobs and crushing destitution, I saw a lack of life, a lack of blood and vitality, which in my head was only to be found in cities, with their threat of danger and violence and privation— the same cities my people had run from. Later I found this same authenticity, this same sense of vitality, in fighting, which my ancestors had sworn off as soon as they had the chance, just like they had the ghettos. My people had wisely and with great effort and over hundreds of years finally freed themselves from trouble. Now here I am, making it for myself.

Early on in my time at Gleason's Gym I meet David Lawrence, a seventy-year-old trainer and writer who looks fifty-five. Short but sinewy and without an ounce of fat on his body, David walks with the permanently rolled-over shoulders of the longtime boxer and a halting gait that suggests neurological slowdown. When he's not instructing some student at the heavy bag or locked away in his office writing, David does hundreds of push-ups and pull-ups, in defiance of his age. When we talk he stutters a bit and often forgets earlier conversations and loses threads, the result of years of hard sparring and fighting. His brain has paid the price for all that bodily perfection.

David first started training at Gleason's when he was thirty-eight years old and chairman and CEO of an insurance broker-age that occupied the entire floor of an office building on Wall Street during the 1980s. He used to ride to the gym in the back of a Rolls-Royce limousine back when Gleason's was still in Manhattan, near Madison Square Garden. He had a Ph.D. in literature. He wrote poems. He made millions of dollars a year. He had everything.

But, like me, David felt hemmed in by the boundaries of Jewish decency and progress. And he felt suffocated by the soft, quiet life of the successful businessman. He longed to live roughly and at a great physical cost, in contention with other men and with himself. So he sought out the strenuous life in boxing. And he found in the world of fighting some authenticity he couldn't locate in his well-heeled, much-respected, profitable but passive life of Jewish propriety. All that righteousness can wear down a man's soul and do him in.

Over the course of his ten-year career David developed a fighting style that reflected these desires and suited his life phi-losophy, one based entirely on offense and abandon. "My defense was good but so what?" he wrote in his 2012 memoir, *The King of White-Collar Boxing.* "Fighting was about hurting and getting hurt." Dorrius would be horrified to read such a thing. After several amateur fights David went pro in his forties and fought until he was fifty, despite suffering separated shoulders, broken noses, and permanent brain damage that wiped out his short-term memory and altered his ability to discern spatial relation-ships, making it all but impossible to keep fighting. And yet he did. Friends and colleagues thought he was crazy for throwing away his life and risking his valuable brain in the ring, but he saw fighting as the "touchstone that made my life meaningful." Coaches and promoters and gym managers and doctors tried to get him to stop before he did more harm to himself, but he didn't mind that he was brain damaged. He saw it as a badge of honor, proof he "did something enthusiastically enough to get hurt." He described his first fight as his second bar mitzvah: a rebirth.

In 1916 the infamous poet and provocateur Arthur Cravan fought former world heavyweight boxing champion Jack Johnson in an exhibition bout in Barcelona, Spain. At the time, Johnson was arguably the greatest heavyweight ever, while Cravan's achievements as a boxer amounted to little more than declaring himself the light heavyweight champion of France after he was the only person to show up at a rookie boxing competition in Paris a year earlier. But this was just like Cravan, who was a proud nephew of Oscar Wilde, another great literary provocateur and self-promoter: to create his life as he saw fit, outside the bounds of convention, and turn living itself into art. Though little known now, Cravan was a hero to early-twentieth-century experimentalists, expanding the whole notion of what constituted art. His experiments in conceptual art and serial transgression influenced the Surrealists, the Dadaists, the Situationists, and any other twentieth-century art movement interested in blurring the line between performer and spectator and between life and art.

Cravan would show up at gallery openings just to shout down the artists. He gave lectures drunk, stripping himself naked as he talked. He wrote wild, hallucinatory dialogues between himself and his late uncle Oscar for his short-lived and scandalous literary journal, *Maintenant*, and used its pages as a venue to humiliate his fellow writers. In his poem "Hie," Cravan declared himself "all man and all animals," beyond the ability of convention and tradition to define: "Man of fashion, chemist, whore, drunk, musician, labourer, painter, acrobat, actor. Old man, child, crook, hooligan, angel and rake; millionaire, bourgeois, cactus, giraffe, or crow; Coward, hero, negro, monkey, Don Juan, pimp, lord, peasant, hunter, industrialist, Flora and fauna."

Cravan's reason for fighting Johnson was, like his life, full of contradictions: courageous and corrupt at once, ideological and self-obsessed. The poet had shown up in Barcelona destitute, after leaving Paris to avoid conscription in the British army, which by that time was deep into World War I. A born conscientious objector who declared he'd rather "break American jaws than face German bayonets," Cravan agreed to fight Johnson (who was also down on his luck after fleeing racially motivated criminal charges in his native America and losing his belt a year earlier to Jess Willard) to earn enough money to buy a boat ticket to New York and avoid military service. Their fight lasted six rounds, with Cravan clinging desperately to the former champion and keeping himself out of punching range, before Johnson finally got one solid punch in, at which point Cravan fell to the canvas in a heap, setting off a riot among the small crowd, which had decided (correctly, it turns out) that the fix was in. Cravan slipped out a side door and was soon aboard the *Montserrat* sailing for New York alongside several other deserters and dissidents, including Russian Communist leader Leon Trotsky.

A fighting poet! For decades writers have been admiring Ernest Hemingway and George Plimpton for dabbling their way through a friendly sparring round or two, barely risking a thing, when all along there was a writer out there who had the courage to fight Jack Johnson and the temerity to declare himself the champion of Europe. A man who fought to free himself from the weight of national history and personal identity, and for art! Why is Arthur Cravan's birthday not celebrated every year in

elementary schools and fighting gyms across America? Where
are the statues and parades?

One day after our training session, Dorrius tells me a story
about knocking out a stranger who was bullying people outside
the turnstiles of a subway station near his apartment in eastern
Brooklyn a few years earlier. There's little visually intimidating
about Dorrius, and this man must have taken one look at his
round belly and short stature and graying hair and decided he
was nothing. But while the man laid into him with insults and
threats, too boorish and self-deluded to notice he was goading
a real fighter, Dorrius was subtly shifting his feet into boxing
position.

Dorrius shows me a garishly misplaced knuckle on his right
hand, the result of one punch to the man's chin and the botched
surgery Dorrius underwent afterward. I had no idea knuckles
could sit that close to the wrist. It turns my stomach to see it.
"You knocked him out with just one punch?" I ask with wonder
and envy, turning my eyes away from his hand. "My fists are can-
nons," Dorrius responds with a grin.

5.

MEMENTO MORI

(SIX MONTHS OUT)

At the very moment I need to be at my most motivated and enthusiastic about this fight, as full of conviction and free of doubt as a religious zealot in the throes of new conversion, I'm suddenly plagued by uncertainty.

This week, at a small MMA event in Dublin, Ireland, a Portuguese mixed martial artist died from head trauma suffered in the cage. One minute he was recovering from a rough but seemingly unexceptional technical knockout, congratulating his opponent and shrugging off medical attention, and the next, this twenty-eight-year-old in the prime of his life, this picture of health and strength, built to withstand and administer awful things, was being rushed to a hospital for emergency brain surgery. Forty-eight hours later he was dead, and a pall descended on the mixed martial arts world.

Any time a fighter dies, his death ripples out and blankets the entire world of fighting in introspection. Fighters turn in

on themselves, growing reflective and philosophical. Hardened
men and women who long ago became numb to the dangers of
fighting, to the blood and bruises and broken limbs, to the moral
ambiguity, men and women who have accepted and forgotten
about the risks of a life spent inviting and inflicting great bodily
harm, suddenly find themselves forced to think about nothing
else and to contemplate the absurdity of their desires. Because
no one who fights even once can hear about a fellow fighter dying from injuries suffered in the cage and fail to imagine him- or
herself in their place. The silent insanity at the heart of fighting,
the thing we all pretend isn't there, that always-lingering reality,
is suddenly impossible to ignore.

And so an unknown Portuguese mixed martial artist becomes a reminder of our individual mortality and testimony to
the inexpressible and unsnappable bonds that tie humanity together, a lesson in universal experience, like some Walt Whitman poem about the interconnectedness of one soul to every
other: "For every atom belonging to me as good belongs to you."
How can I not think about my own atoms when faced with the
vanishing of another's, especially one who vanished doing the
very thing I've declared myself self-destructive enough to do?

The first fighter to die in a sanctioned MMA bout in North
America was a Texan named Sam Vasquez. After getting
knocked down in the third round of a fight on October 20, 2007,
in Houston, Vasquez collapsed in the cage, at which point a subdural hemorrhage began to develop on the left side of his brain.
After Vasquez was admitted to the hospital the swelling began
to shift toward the right side, requiring emergency surgery to
remove a portion of his skull. According to the autopsy report,
two weeks later Vasquez suffered a "sudden decline in neurologi-

cal status" and was fitted with a catheter to drain cerebral spinal fluid in an attempt to reduce swelling in his brain. He died on November 30.

In March 2014, Congolese fighter Booto Guylain died one week after suffering a head injury in the third round of a fight in Johannesburg, South Africa. The cause of death, again, was complications from swelling in the brain.

South Korean mixed martial artist Lee died following an unsanctioned fight in Samsong-dong, an upscale neighborhood in Seoul, in May 2005. Doctors declared the official cause of death to be myocardial infarction.

Douglas Dedge died on March 18, 1998, of "severe brain injuries" after competing at an unsanctioned event in Kiev, Ukraine, two days earlier. The thirty-one-year-old is believed to be the first American fatally injured in an MMA fight.

Azerbaijani Ramin Zeynalov died in the cage after getting knocked out during a national tournament in March 2014. Medical personnel on the scene were unable to revive Zeynalov, who, it was later determined, died from a brain hemorrhage.

Jameston Lee-Yaw, a Trinidad-born kickboxer turned mixed martial artist, died two days after collapsing in the ring during an amateur fight at a shopping mall in Aberdeen, Washington. The King County Medical Examiner's Office reported the cause of death as kidney failure. The event was not required to have medical staff present, but a representative of the gym that put on the fight said Lee-Yaw had "passed his prefight check with flying colors." Lee-Yaw was forty-seven years old, an ancient in the fighting world.

The symptoms of brain trauma can be so subtle at first that the crowd and even a fighter's coaches may not notice them, or they may just take them for signs of fatigue. The fighter may start to stumble as he moves around the cage. He may drop his hands and reach for the fence to steady himself, even when he's in the center of the cage. His reaction time and eye-hand coordination slow down. He starts to feel disoriented and confused. His feet, trained to move parallel and in concert, begin to cross, leaving him off-balance and vulnerable to his opponent's attacks. This lack of coordination is known as a gait disturbance; ring doctors are trained to look out for it as an early-warning sign of brain injury. When the bell rings to end the round, the fighter may stagger back to his corner like he's had too much to drink, and when he sits down on his stool he may have trouble holding up his head or focusing his eyes. His coach is yelling, urging him to fight through what he assumes is just exhaustion, but the fighter is unable to concentrate on what his coach is saying or even respond to simple commands. The coach raises his fighter's head up so he can take a drink of water and lifts him back to his feet for the last round, but by now he can't stand on his own. He may collapse to the canvas before the round even begins.

One of the clearest signs of severe cranial trauma and subdural bleeding is the inability of the pupil to react to light, so the first thing the doctor will do upon entering the ring after a fighter collapses is shine a flashlight in his eyes. If his pupil doesn't constrict in response, it means he's likely suffered neurological damage. Time is of the essence now. Both concussions and subdural hemorrhaging can lead to swelling of the brain, compression of brain tissue, and increased intracranial pressure. When the brain swells inside the confined space of the skull, it can be forced down the spinal cord, pushing up against the brain stem. This herniation can lead to a loss of all involuntary brain stem reflexes (including gagging and blinking), cardiac arrest, coma, respiratory arrest, and organ failure.

If the swelling in the fighter's brain is severe enough, surgeons may have to perform a ventriculostomy, cutting a small hole in the skull and inserting a tube to drain cerebrospinal fluid from the brain. If that doesn't work they may have to remove part of his skull to relieve the intracranial pressure, a procedure known as a decompressive craniectomy.

Maybe the damaged fighter doesn't show any symptoms at all. This is possible with acute intracranial bleeding and other head trauma. He fights a whole fight and walks around the cage afterward like nothing's wrong, talking to his coaches, even congratulating his opponent. No one notices any problem, not even the doctor. Only later will he begin deteriorating, after he's left the ring, or when he's back in the locker room. Maybe that's where he'll finally collapse.

Following an amateur fight in Mount Pleasant, South Carolina, in August 2012, Tyrone Mims, a thirty-year-old Georgia native, collapsed in the venue and died at the hospital an hour later. At the time doctors had no idea what killed Mims—there was no evidence of head trauma or kidney failure or myocardial infarction—and after a three-month investigation that included a complete forensic autopsy, toxicology testing, and genetic testing, the Charleston County Coroner's office was forced to admit that the cause of death was undetermined. "At this point in time, we have exhausted all that we know to do," coroner Rae Wooten said when the report was released. "There's just nothing here that explains his death."

How terrible to die without the dignity of a scientific explanation, a mystery beyond the powers of medicine to comprehend. Thousands of years of accumulated human knowledge and death can still happen for no reason at all. It can just steal us away—like some unnameable specter, like a looming childhood menace that never goes away. The inescapable menace. What an epitaph: "There's just nothing here that explains his death."

Most of my toes are bent and sore from slamming into other people's knees and shins and elbows. My feet hurt to walk on. My thighs are constantly battered from kicks, my biceps perpetually bruised from grappling sessions. Hip inflexibility, exacerbated by innumerable roundhouse kicks thrown into countless heavy bags and by having my legs wrenched open by jiujitsu players looking to pass my guard, makes it difficult to walk down stairs with any grace or speed. Like an old man, I approach them at a forty-five-degree angle. Bursitis in my left clavicle, which I never allow the time to heal because I can't bear to be away from fighting that long and instead aggravate daily with push-ups and private lessons with Muay Thai masters who initiate me into the mysteries of the upper-body clinch by wrenching my neck and shoulders in impossible directions and then dumping my body violently to the mat, clavicle first, makes it difficult to reach too far over my head. Only forty years old and I limp everywhere and have trouble scratching my own back. I think fighting is simultaneously slowing down and accelerating the aging process. I feel like a million dollars and a broken-down car.

This is the great paradox of fighting: Fighters seek to defy death by destroying life, and in return they feel more alive. The body (life's stand-in), subjected to punches and kicks and chokes and wrenching joint locks, is torn apart by fighting but thrives because of it. This is a cliché, of course. Self-creation through self-destruction is something of a silent mantra in the fighting world, understood by every fighter no matter how subconsciously. We feel worse when we're *not* in any pain. Fighting teaches you to dive deep down into the full experience of life, where even misery is pleasurable, because to be alive is to be happy, and to court death is to thumb your nose at it, and to live.

In the late ninth century the Benedictine monk and poet Notker of Saint Gall saw workers building a bridge over a great abyss and was inspired to write down the line *Media vita in morte sumus*. In the midst of life we are in death. This sentiment was eventually enshrined in the Anglican Book of Common Prayer and its author beatified in 1512 by Pope Julius II. But fighters know Notker had it backward. In the midst of death we are in life.

Joel Rosenblatt died on December 3, 2006, at the age of sixty-two, after collapsing in the hallway of his small one-bedroom apartment in suburban Maryland. He was found next to a stack of unopened moving boxes, though he had lived in that apartment for at least a year. No autopsy was performed, but the cause of death could have been any number of ailments, both physical and emotional, both real and imagined, that had plagued him for decades: heart trouble, diabetes, obesity, depression, loneliness, existential dread, perpetual disappointment, acute hypochondria. Or his death could have been caused by the ever-shifting cocktail of prescription drugs he took to combat those illnesses. My father carried the contents of a small pharmacy around in his veins at all times. *His* delusion was that life and death could be fortified against, that they were conditions to be treated. Fighting is something he never would have done because fighting is all about blood and risk and pain and recovery: the whole cycle is required. My father was terrified of pain and even more terrified of recovery. His identity was wrapped up in his suffering.

In a strange twist of fate, my fight has been scheduled for the week after the tenth anniversary of my father's death. This is just a coincidence, but it makes me wonder whether in some way this fighting obsession is my response to the cerebral, soft, drug-addled, doctor-populated, fearful, paralyzed, inward life he led and that I'm always in danger of falling into if I'm not careful: my inheritance. My father, for all his intellect and humor and capacity for compassion, was locked inside himself, trapped in failure and the premonition and daily approximation of his own death, the very thing he feared so much. And I, the good son, perpetually in danger of being swallowed by similar demons, am always raging against that fate. Hence fighting: the lousiest possible refuge for an interior soul.

"Death is the mother of beauty," the poet Wallace Stevens wrote. "Hence from her, / Alone, shall come fulfilment to our dreams / And our desires."

Or maybe I'm being dramatic. Now that my fight is becoming a reality, it's possible I'm romanticizing the metaphorical specter of death to hide my fear of *actual* death. But I have to shake free of that. The romance of fighting belongs to spectators and screenwriters. There should be no poetry for the fighter. That kind of abstract thinking will only get you hurt. To fight is to face cold realities.

But to fight is also to tap into dark and elemental forces. MMA isn't just a sport—it's a means of summoning spirits, of tempting incomprehensible powers and teasing them, daring them to work on you. It's about finding pleasure in creating suffering, enhancing life while conjuring death. Fighting allows otherwise ordinary twenty-first-century human beings to mingle with prehistoric calamity and destruction, to witness the endless human battle between savage impulse and civilizing intention, between the evolved brain and the instinctual, between society and older, more sinister forces of black magic.

Though you never hear about this side of the sport from those involved. Talk to fighters and coaches and pundits and you'll hear inspiring speeches about discipline and self-improvement and artistry and nobility and will and respect and strength of character and soundness of body and honor—so much honor!— but there's always that darker something bubbling just below the surface. Doesn't there have to be, when you're playing around with real bodily harm and, yes, even death? When you're messing with darkness and internal mystery and madness and the primordial menace we spring from and confronting the fear of what's inside yourself, not knowing what you're capable of in the throes of violent confrontation or how deep and far your own psychoses go, not when you've never allowed them full and free expression before, when they've only been able to seep into the world subliminally, in metaphorical dribs and drabs? How strange and liberating to find a popular art form in the enlightened twenty-first century whose highest realization requires tapping into our basest instincts and causing harm to other human beings. How many times have I marveled during fighting classes at the countless hours and boundless intellectual energy that must have gone into developing and fine-tuning ways to harm our fellow man—all the imagination we've employed to destroy ourselves. What an evolution.

For every Douglas Dedge there's a Yevgeni Zolotarev. For every Booto Guylain there's a Keron Davies. For every Tyrone Mims there's a Blake Poore. For every fighter who dies in a cage there's another who contributed to the death. And while there may be romance in risking your own life for the sake of an experience, to dabble in homicide presents an entirely different kind of risk. One imperils the body, the other imperils the soul.

As I get closer to my fight a question keeps forcing its way into my head, pestering me when I'm on the treadmill or punching the heavy bag or trying to visualize my techniques and strategies: Do I have it in me to hurt somebody? Do I actually *want* to hurt somebody? Deep down, am I *pining* to hurt somebody?

Norman Mailer once wrote that fighting "arouses two of the deepest anxieties we contain. There is not only the fear of getting hurt, which is profound in more men than will admit to it, but there is the opposite panic, equally unadmitted, of hurting others." But there's a third anxiety Mailer failed to mention, maybe the worst of them all: the terror of discovering in the middle of a fight that you *enjoy* hurting others. That's what worries me.

For forty years I've buried any instincts I have toward violence under an ever-growing edifice of civility, decency, passivity, lust, cowardice, sublimation, intellectualism, and irony. But the personal anger we accrue over a lifetime of disappointments and emotional scars and the primordial, ancestral instincts toward violence we all share, passed down over millions of years, don't just quietly drift away. They're always there, waiting to burst their civilizing chains.

Recently a good friend told me he wouldn't be coming to my fight for this very reason. This friend, a filmmaker and musician, may not have an ounce of the fighting spirit in him, but, like me, he's fascinated by the degradations of the flesh and the lofty desires of the spirit and the delicate dance between the two. So when he told me he couldn't bear to watch me fight, I assumed it was because he didn't want to see me get beaten up, but it turns out the opposite is true. He's terrified at the prospect of seeing me *win*, of seeing my punches land on another man's face and the look in my eye when they do, of witnessing the unleashed id of a man he's known for twenty years, someone he eats lunch with, someone who plays with his kids. I'd never thought about this. I'd never considered the possibility that by transforming myself into a fighter I'll be putting on display some part of me no one else was ever meant to see—that sinister, amoral, sadistic, bloodthirsty part that I know intimately but that's supposed to stay tucked away for civilization's sake. Every man has a demon inside, but not every man is reckless enough to expose that demon to his friends and family, to risk inspiring their terror and disgust.

In nineteenth-century Gothic novels, every doctor who dares to dabble in the monstrous side of the human beast for knowledge's sake is punished. Dr. Jekyll. Dr. Moreau. Dr. Frankenstein. Exploration into the mysteries and limits of the human body and the depths of human darkness always comes with a terrible and lasting price: distortion of one's humanity, the loathing of your fellow man, self-banishment. Does something similar happen to a fighter after he's spent years rewiring his brain and rearranging neural pathways in order to overcome his fear and ignore that most fundamental human instinct, the instinct toward self-preservation, and the most basic human sympathy? Does he become something different then? Something other? Something less than human? Something monstrous?

In high-stress situations the body releases cortisol, a steroid hormone produced in the adrenal glands, into the blood, which car-

ries it throughout the body and across the blood-brain barrier.
Of the receptors in the brain that cortisol acts on, one seems to
enhance plasticity, the other to impair it. Which means when
a person is exposed to chronic stress and the brain is flooded
with cortisol, some areas of the brain can grow while others
shrink. The hippocampus, the region of the brain where memories are stored and processed, contains many cortisol receptors
and under repeated stress has been shown to atrophy, resulting
in significant memory loss. Since the hippocampus is also involved in the regulation of the brain's stress response, the shrinking caused by chronic stress and heavy cortisol production can
weaken and impair the brain's natural feedback loop, meaning
the brain's response to stress gets even more exaggerated because
the mechanism regulating that response has been impaired.

One area of the brain that can *expand* in response to that
extra cortisol is the amygdala, the ancient area of the brain dealing with emotions. Neurons in the amygdala can branch out
and grow more synapses as a result of the presence of excessive
cortisol, enhancing the brain's capacity for fear and aggression
and other instinctual, defensive responses. So, if fighters could
be said to live in a perpetual state of fight-or-flight, a sort of low-
grade chronic stress, it's possible that they're forever growing
that primordial, unregulated, aggressive, fear-driven region of
the brain we share with even the lowliest beasts of the jungle.

So, the question sits there: Is there real violence in me? And if so,
what will happen when I crack myself open to let it out? Will I
be able to just tuck it back down again once the fight is over, snuff
it out and pretend it was never there, as if I'd merely dabbled
in a frame of mind, like some psychological dilettante, like an
emotional tourist, before returning to a life of quiet decency?

Or will something dormant get stirred up in me and refuse to be put back down to sleep? Am I risking damage far beyond the physical here? Am I messing with ghosts and forces I shouldn't be? Is my soul in peril? What if I become a monster? And what if I like it?

6

THIS FRAGILE FORM

(FOUR MONTHS OUT)

When I first heard the pop I wasn't sure what had happened; there was no pain, just the feeling that something had gone terribly wrong. My jiujitsu sparring partner—a born optimist— blamed his judo *gi*. He told me he had torn it some months before while training and now every so often, during a particularly heated sparring session, the tear will grow bigger. "That must have been it," he said hopefully. "Shall we continue?"

But he knew as well as I did that the sound had come not from his stitching but from my right hand, which had gotten caught in the lapel of his *gi* as he was attempting to break my grip. I was in his guard (he supine, me on my knees facing him, with his legs wrapped around my back) attempting to stand up and free myself. To do this I needed to keep my right hand gripped on his lapel to control him and prevent him from having any mobility. His job, meanwhile, was to break that grip. To my mind, though, in doing so he had snatched my hand with an unnecessary amount of force while thrusting his chest upward with a gratuitous amount of strength, creating a vise that wrenched my hand at a terrible angle. Had we been fighting for real this move would have been masterful, something I would have admired even through my pain and disappointment, but we were only sparring, and even in those first stages of physical panic I judged his actions as unsporting. *No, we won't be continuing today.*

I reached over with my left hand (which had been trying to control his sleeve when the pop happened) and felt the base knuckle on my right middle finger moving around unnaturally where it connects with the bone at the top of the palm, accompanied by just the slightest clicking sound. That's when the pain started, as if my body had been waiting for recognition from the brain. At first it was light, barely noticeable beneath the numbness and agitation. Then my middle finger began to throb and a shock shot down the back of my hand toward the wrist. I told my partner I'd had enough for the day and got myself out from between his legs and off the mat.

Back in the locker room my hand was swelling up quickly, and the simplest tasks were already becoming difficult. Removing my sweat-soaked T-shirt was excruciating; putting on my socks and opening my water bottle were a torment. Every time I gripped my hand a surge of pain shot through it and up my arm. My middle base knuckle was in less pain now, just slightly sore to the touch, but it seemed to be unmoored, moving around and popping each time I flexed my fingers. After agonizing myself into my sneakers I sat quietly for a moment on the locker room bench to contemplate my new reality.

I knew I would need to see my doctor. But what would I tell him? He had already scheduled me for X-rays later that week to figure out the source of new pain in my hips and shoulder, and now this? Could I ask for a third? Four months from my fight, my body was collapsing on at least three fronts and my training was really just getting going. Who knows what other small irritations and great horrors lay in store?

As I walked to the subway, holding my hand close to my chest to avoid being banged into by some unknowing Midtown tourist or a businessman pushing his way toward Penn Station after a long day's work, I marveled, really for the first time, at the countless stories I'd heard about mixed martial artists fighting through injuries: sprained ankles and twisted arms and busted knees and broken hands and shattered noses and partially severed ears and battered thighs and compound fractures and hideously bent fingers and garish hematomas and eyebrow lacerations and eyes swollen shut and gushing blood. Among fighters it's understood that only the most hideous and life-threatening injuries should be conceded to, and those only begrudgingly. They're a proud group. And with each step up Seventh Avenue, my respect for them was growing in direct proportion to my pain.

On the train ride home, I started to feel paralyzed, physically and psychologically. Black thoughts were beginning to form, working their way past the pain and metastasizing into early panic. I knew even then I'd need to stop training, but for how long? And would I be able to write in the meantime, or would even typing be too much? I need them both. Fighting is my reprieve from the cerebral agonies of writing, and writing is my civilizing response to the monstrous demands of fighting; they keep each other balanced, like two sides of a split personality. And working together, fighting and writing keep my most antisocial inclinations in check. What if they were both taken away? Who knows what I'd be capable of, what tendencies I'd revert to? I saw dark clouds gathering.

———

In addition to the pain and swelling, the middle finger of my right hand is now burrowed slightly under the ring finger, where before there was space between the two. My doctor tells me this is either the result of a ruptured tendon in the middle finger or swelling due to a fracture. Extensor tendons run the length of the hand, connecting the small bones of the fingers to the muscles of the arm, which make the fingers move. At the base of each finger, attached to these main flexor tendons, are smaller branches that connect to the muscles in the back of the hand, known as the dorsal interossei, that control the spreading of the fingers. These smaller tendons are like the ropes keeping a tent tied to the ground. When one side is severed from the muscle, the attached finger will collapse to the opposite side, where it's still connected, and lean against the neighboring finger. My doctor calls this sudden nuzzling of the middle and ring fingers my "deformity."

If there is a fracture but the two segments of the bone are still aligned, a month or six weeks in a splint should heal me. If the bone segments aren't aligned, however, if displacement has occurred, or if my tendons have in fact ruptured, then surgery will likely be necessary (including the insertion of pins to realign the bone), which means I could be on the shelf for months. It's now the last week in August. My fight is scheduled for December.

The spiritual father of Brazilian jiujitsu, Hélio Gracie, grew up an invalid in Rio de Janeiro, the youngest and frailest of five brothers. As a child he would faint after running up a flight of stairs. While his brothers trained and taught Japanese jiujitsu, Hélio, under doctor's orders, would sit and watch. When he finally started training at age sixteen, Hélio began adapting what he'd seen to accommodate his physical limitations and weaknesses, coming up with a new martial art that emphasized leverage and timing over strength and speed. By its nature Brazilian jiujitsu was a martial art designed for the physically vulnerable, and its entire aim was to capitalize on the vulnerability of others.

All the times I visualized getting injured in the cage, I never imagined this. I had pictured concussions, of course, and fractured arms and bruised thighs and broken noses, because those injuries are the predictable consequences of fighting; they may even be one of fighting's primary aims. While causing injuries in a fight may fall lower on the humanist's list of priorities than winning, to deny the pain-causing intentions in mixed martial arts in the name of nobility and athleticism is to ignore the cruelty at its heart. Punches break noses and cause concussions. *Kimura* locks break arms. Leg kicks smash nerves. Bodies ruin other bodies.

But no one is out to break an opponent's metacarpal bone or rupture her extensor digitorum tendon when they attempt a jiujitsu sweep. No one even contemplates the possibility. They're just hoping to work themselves free from a bad position. But the dangers of Brazilian jiujitsu are inscrutable and everywhere. Black belts can submit their opponents by attacking ankles, elbows, necks, knees, even waists, wrapping them into knots and turning their own bodies against them. They use leverage and balance to upset equilibrium, create a sense of panic in the body, and punish their opponents for the most habitual, seemingly insignificant gestures: touch your hand to the ground for just a moment and you risk getting caught in an armbar, stand with your feet side by side for a second too long and you'll be swept onto your back, stand up the way a normal person stands up and before you know it you're in a guillotine choke and the world is turning black around you.

And the same way Brazilian jiujitsu has expanded the boundaries of what can be done in a fight, of what we think of a fight even being, it's expanded the palette of injuries that can end one as well. When a fighting style is built around making every part of the human body vulnerable, it shouldn't come as a surprise when any part of the body gets mangled.

Yet I'm surprised. And shaken. Unimaginable perils lurk everywhere in grappling, and when you get swamped by one you can lose faith in your understanding of the world and the stability of your place in it. This is now happening to me. For the first time since I started fighting, I can feel the confidence draining out of me, like a sorcerer realizing too late that the forces he's conjured are of a strength and magnitude beyond his ability to control. The randomness and implausibility of this injury are conspiring to make me feel vulnerable. I realize now—I feel it deep down—that any part of me can fall apart at any time. Because of a fluke run-in with another man's lapel, I feel exposed, taught a lesson by a cruel and indifferent universe.

"So, is there a point at which your responsibility to me as my doctor and to your oath is to *not* treat me, but rather to chide me for my willfulness and my indifference to my health and to all your labors to keep my body intact, to *refuse* to treat me until I agree to stop mauling myself like this, and then send me on my way? A bit of tough love? Wouldn't that be the more reasonable, more humane thing to do?"

My doctor smiles: the wise physician gazing down from his perch on the confused patient.

"If that were a treatment option, then all patients who show up with drug overdoses would be turned out," he says. "But we don't, because we know too well that seventy-five percent of people who overdose on drugs and who need help we'll see again at some point down the road. Addiction is one of those scenarios where people are doing things that are clearly putting themselves in harm's way, but that doesn't mean we stop helping them. And if we continue to keep treating *them* we'll continue to keep treating *you*, whose self-harm is unfolding on a much smaller scale, though equally stubborn." And with that he laughs and hands me a referral for an X-ray to go with the others before ushering me out of his office.

Did he just call me an addict?

A personal inventory, ten years in: seven broken toes, five dislocated fingers, three black eyes, dozens of bloody noses, perpetually sore knees, permanently bruised shins, split lips, countless headaches, six probable concussions, three herniated discs, two impacted toenails, one lightly misshapen nose, minor cauliflower ear, one case of shoulder bursitis, two less-than-mobile hips, one busted hand.

Oscar Wilde: "The life that was to make his soul would mar his body."

I know now that my doctors won't stop me from fighting no matter what I do to myself over the next three months. Neither will the X-ray technician at the hospital, a former NYPD detective with a thick Brooklyn accent who, when I tell him why he has to take X-rays of my hips, my shoulder, *and* my hand on the same day, lights up. "My son is in Arizona training MMA!" he tells me. Then, leaning in closer to adjust my radiation protection vest and move the collimator from my left shoulder to my right hand, he looks at me and laughs: "I'm worried about him, sure, but there are worse things he could be doing: fighting on the streets or doing drugs. Worst-case scenario, you get your ass kicked and learn something about yourself, right?"

That's it? A bit of self-knowledge? That's what a medical professional has to say about my voluntary courtship of major injury? I wanted him to tell me I was being ridiculous, that no forty-year-old should be getting X-rays on three different parts of his body at once, that I didn't have to do this. My body keeps sending me warning signals telling me to get out of this fight, and the medical world keeps sending me enablers. *Why won't someone tell me to stop? Will no one save me from myself?*

According to my X-ray report, printed on August 25, 2016, by New York Methodist Hospital in Brooklyn, I have suffered an "oblique fracture through the third metacarpal shaft in good alignment."

This is the best diagnosis I could have hoped for, short of hypochondria. Yes, I've broken the bone that connects my middle finger to my wrist, but the two segments of the shaft (the body of the bone) are still in line with each other, meaning that as the bone heals, it will return to its natural shape without the help of surgery or the insertion of pins. The threat of three months away from the gym and a delay of my fight has vanished. My doctor prescribes six weeks in a splint before returning to full-contact training. I'm so relieved I could cry. I can handle six weeks away.

Within a week I'm going mad. I don't know if it's that I've grown accustomed to the adrenaline or the endorphins or the risk-taking or the violence or simply having a reason to leave the house every day, but my years of training have left me unprepared for all this passivity. After just a week of inaction I'm finding myself in deep waters of deflation. I don't know how to occupy myself. I need fighting in my life the way some people need God or drugs, and now my hand and the fates are conspiring against me.

The old, prefighting me would have celebrated having six weeks of doctor-ordered indolence. But now I might get swallowed up in brooding if I'm not careful. If fighting breeds a certain pleasant narcissism, a mild obsession with the development of one's own body and a growing fascination with the thrill of indestructibility, it also, by its nature, requires contact with other people, not to mention a deeper sense of humanity through shared fragility. Fighting puts you in touch with others even as you're attempting their domination. But passivity and isolation breed solipsism, dragging you down into the mire of the self, where every surface reflects back on itself. The great peril of inactivity is that you become convinced that the world is actually revolving around you but to no purpose. In the fighting world, the fear of injury, the constant reaffirmation of inability, and the required presence of other people don't allow for any morbid self-fascination.

Without the rituals of the gym, without the thrills of sparring and the mind-soothing endorphins that come with it—the chemical reward—life is quickly growing gray and dull again, and my body and mind are seeking out substitutes: bursts of sensual indulgence to compensate for the sudden lack of discipline. Old inclinations from my prefighting life are starting to rattle around in my brain again, calling me back. Because vice and virtue are two sides of the same coin, just like self-creation and self-destruction.

To make matters worse, learning to fight rouses ancient lusts and instincts. When you suddenly stop fighting, the in-

stinct for destruction and the lust for violence don't just disappear. Like energy, they merely get transferred elsewhere. They
turn inward. All your newfound talent for human ruination and
violence and destruction is now turned on yourself. You begin
to tear yourself apart as only you know how. Because you know
all your weakest points, where you're most vulnerable. So you
drink and you smoke and you eat and your mind wanders and
you dream of other women and you return to your basest habits
and the seductive delights of morbid dissipation. All that lovely
and inspiring self-improvement distorted into solipsism and debasement. Anything to relieve the ungodly boredom.

Before I broke my hand, the longest time I'd spent away from
fighting was six miserable, dormant weeks after voluntary surgery to fix a deviated septum five years ago. I don't remember
much from those six weeks except that they were filled with
television and whiskey and nothingness, dreary days and grim
nights. When my doctor finally allowed me to start training
again, I was so anxious for any kind of action that I foolishly
agreed to a sparring session after my first class back at the gym.
This was a terrible idea. My reflexes were sluggish and my body
was soft and the man I'd agreed to fight hadn't taken the previous six weeks off. I was exhausted almost as soon as our sparring session started. All of his strikes got through my defense. I
gave nothing in return. A few minutes in, he kicked me in the
nose and I started to bleed everywhere—all over my shirt and
the mat, even the wall I banged into. After stumbling to the
bathroom and examining my swelling nose in the mirror, I realized it had taken me less than five minutes to break what it had
taken a surgeon, centuries of accumulated medical knowledge,
and most of the money I had to mend. But better that, I thought,

better the pain and the embarrassment and the poverty, than the aimless misery the previous month and a half had been. If my septum had been redeviated by that kick, so be it. I wasn't going back to that other life.

Sir Arthur Conan Doyle called fighting the "blessed safety-valve" through which a person's "jangled nerves might find some outlet." Lord Byron wrote about fighting and other similarly "unpoetical exercises" as a balm for his spirit. He even sparred on the day of his mother's funeral. Ten days after injuring my hand, I can't stand my jangled nerves and the boredom and quiet of my apartment any longer, so I rush back to the gym, ignoring my doctor, my coaches, and my own better judgment. Hope without an object cannot live, after all, and a solid punch to the nose cures all psychic ills.

When I arrive at the gym I beg Dorrius to come up with a training regimen that will take into account my battered right hand. Whether we concentrate on my jab or my footwork or my head movement or my defense or my cardiovascular fitness, I don't care—I need to get back to training or else I'm going to run mad. I can't just sit around for the next five weeks while my hand recovers, drowning in misery. I need to keep my reflexes and fighting instincts sharp and my body in shape and, more important, keep the beast at bay, before decay can sink into depravity and depravity can melt into depression and depression seeks self-medication in more depravity. Before this lovely exercise in insanity becomes unsalvageable.

While I'm warming up on the treadmill that first day back I see my friend Howard, a sixty-nine-year-old lawyer who looks like George Plimpton and who fought his first amateur match when he was sixty-five. Howard is always at the gym, either training or gabbing, as genial and generous a person as you could hope to meet. But today he's dressed in street clothes and he looks pale and gaunt, nothing at all like the rangy fighter I've watched stab at the heavy bag on countless occasions or the jovial soul who likes to engage me in conversation *while* we're sparring. He looks exhausted. His eyelids are heavy. He appears to be wandering aimlessly around the gym. I walk over to tell him about the enormous tragedy that's befallen me. Surely Howard will understand.

"I just got out of the hospital," he says before I can tell him about my hand. His voice sounds weak. "I got pneumonia while I was on vacation with my wife in Wisconsin. I was in the intensive care unit for six days. My doctor said if I hadn't gotten to the hospital when I did I could have died."

"My god!" I say, hiding my splinted hand behind my back. "What are you doing back here?" As if I don't know the answer.

"Well, when I was lying there in the ICU I was bored out of my mind," he tells me. "I was scared, but mainly I was bored. The U.S. Open was on TV, but how much tennis can a person watch? All the time I was there I was thinking about fighting, *dreaming* about boxing. On the third day I started getting my strength back and they were letting me walk around the hallways, and I was begging my doctor to let me leave so I could get back here to the gym. I was going nuts without fighting."

I'm starting to feel ashamed of the ten days I took off to rest a hand.

I run into David Lawrence outside his office and show him my splint. "I couldn't stay away," I tell him proudly. I then point to Howard and marvel that he's already back in the gym after his brush with death. "Yeah, boxers are crazy," David says. "I got knocked out in my second fight and I was back in the gym training three days later. Doctors don't recommend that for your brain, but what can you do?"

As soon as I start training again I can feel my despair draining out of me, the clouds lifting. I feel revived and revitalized. And not just because of the endorphins but the sense of possibility, the threat of violence in the air, and the realization that I am back among my people. As I run on the treadmill for the first time in two weeks, watching fighters spar and shadowbox and hit the speed bag, I actually feel my heart well up with contentment.

Accepting Darwin's premise that one must adapt or become obsolete, Dorrius puts me to work perfecting my left hand. The jab is the center of the fighter's world, the heart of his color palette, the core from which all joys and miseries spring. To have a great jab is to have a firm foundation and an artist's tool. But despite its being the most basic and important strike there is, its magic is elusive. Boxers train for years to get a great jab, and most never get there. And you can count the number of mixed martial artists with truly great jabs on two hands, so deep are its mysteries.

Which means this whole metacarpal fiasco could, if I'm lucky, turn out to be a blessing in disguise, all the pain and expense and wasted time and morbidity and boredom an opportunity rather than a burden. Having all this mandated time to concentrate on just my left hand might accelerate my initiation into the mysteries of the jab and prove to be a secret weapon when I fight.

Dorrius works me without any sympathy for the physical and emotional fallout from my injury and indifferent to the fact that I haven't moved a muscle in over a week. I shadowbox and spend long rounds bobbing and weaving under a string. I slam my left hand into the heavy bag and use it to work the speed bag—*bakata bakata bakata*. I practice my fakes and my feints to trick and con my opponent into raising his gloves or attempting to parry my nonexistent punches, and I learn how to move seamlessly from a jab to a left hook to a left uppercut, finding all the ways in and around and up to my opponent's chin. Dorrius, wearing pads on his hands and clad in a great belly pad, stalks me around the ring, calling out combinations and forcing me into corners I then have to dance and jab my way out of. I can feel my left hand becoming a tool, a truly useful instrument.

And all the while my splint-covered right hand just sits there planted at my cheek, unmoving, humbled, and useless—a constant reminder of the fragility of the human body and the frailty of human ambition.

For as long as human beings have been fighting with their hands, they've been throwing wild, winging, round punches at each other. But the development of straight punches came over time, as the result of tactical thought. Straight punches, and particularly the jab, are proof of human evolution. The jab, though less powerful than a cross or a hook or an uppercut, is the quickest of all strikes. The jab is rarely a knockout blow on its own, but it creates the world in which knockouts can occur. The jab keeps opponents off balance and opens doors. A good jab is the sign of a scientific boxer.

Because it's less powerful than a cross, the jab was viewed skeptically by boxers and boxing fans for centuries for being insufficiently masculine, until the late eighteenth century, when John Jackson won the English championship using a jab-heavy style. The son of a builder, Jackson came from a higher social class than most boxers, and he became famous for dressing well, speaking well, and bringing a new air of gentility and sophistication to the otherwise brutish world of prizefighting, as exemplified by his heavy use of the jab. One hundred years later, the American boxer James J. Corbett became the first man to win the heavyweight championship under Marquess of Queensberry Rules (which introduced three-minute rounds, ten-second counts, gloves, and other civilizing delicacies to boxing) by relying on his left jab. At the time boxing was not much different from no-holds-barred fighting, populated, according to former champion Bob Fitzsimmons, by "rough-and-tumble boys." But with his scientific left hand, Corbett revolutionized the sport, turning it into a game of skill and art rather than simple toughness.

John Jackson went by the nickname "The Gentleman Boxer." Corbett was known as "Gentleman Jim." The jab is the punch of the sophisticated.

When I go back to the gym later in the week, Howard is there again. This time, though, he's hitting the heavy bag. The light is back in his eyes and he looks healthy and free. In one week he's transformed himself from a patient on the brink back into a person and finally back into a fighter. He greets me with a big smile and tells me his doctor cleared him to start training again this morning. He says he immediately went home and grabbed his gloves. I could kiss him. He wants to know when I'll be well enough to spar with him again. Soon, I say.

Fighting is both a disease and a cure.

7

THE WATER OF LIFE

(THREE MONTHS OUT)

Six weeks dead and buried! Six miserable, proscribed, bland weeks during which I was forced to reduce fighting to a series of heartless and harmless gestures, to dispassionate technique, six weeks of trying to find satisfaction in jabbing exercises and footwork drills and hip-mobility circuits, anything to keep myself free from the grasp of despair. Pretending that this was enough—that fighting is a sport just like any other, and so when an injury to one part of the body is suffered the slack is simply picked up by others, on stationary bikes and treadmills, that the competitive instinct is sublimated and fighters can still slake their lusts in weightlifting or long runs. But I knew even before I broke that bone in my hand that the desire to hit and be hit by a fellow human being, once pricked into life, can't be satisfied with speed bags or jump ropes. That the lust for grappling finds no relief in plyometric exercise routines. The need to fight can only be satisfied by fighting. Everything else is a lie we tell ourselves to keep from jumping off a bridge when the doctor tells us we have to abstain from what we love best for six weeks or six months or a year. Without the lie we'd be dragged down into despair.

And so, what joy it's going to be to finally dump that lie and walk back into the gym, to remove my stale-smelling splint and toss it into the darkest corner of my closet, to begin sparring again—to give up life as one of the injured and once again take my chances with the dark forces of the fighting ring. The language of rebirth won't be melodramatic then: the moment I return to the cage I will come back to life. O, sweet, sweet recovery of the limbs. O, blessed reconstituted third metacarpal. What a reparative miracle the body is!

But before rebirth, a little touch of self-sabotage.

To celebrate the end of my six-week confinement and the return of my right hand, I decide a night of serious drinking is in order. Surely I've earned it, slogging through the last month and a half without taking a single punch to the face or knee to the solar plexus or tossing another human being to the ground: suffering through the quiet life. So I call up a filmmaker friend of mine who's been going through his own crisis of creative confidence and demand he come out with me, knowing there's no better balm for the suffering soul than drunken commiseration.

By the time I stumble home it's three in the morning. And when I arrive at the gym six hours later, I'm dying a slow death. From the time the warm-up begins I can feel each glass of whiskey rebelling in my blood. Every push-up and every second of jogging on the treadmill is a small misery. I can barely move. This is the downside to developing an intimate and mutually beneficial relationship with your body: you feel more acutely the disconnection when it comes.

The woman I'm sparring with is good, but on most days I would have no trouble with her. She's faster than I am, but I always wear her down with technique and persistence, frustrating her with my long jab and my quick combinations and keeping her far away with quick stabbing kicks at her midsection. But on this, my first day back, I have no will to fight. I drank it all away last night. She easily evades my slow jabs and pops inside my long reach with punches of her own. I'm so tired and distracted, I barely even find the strength or the will to throw my recovered right hand, the whole reason for last night's celebration. Because my reflexes are off, she's able to bend her knees, change levels, and dash in on my body easily, clasping her hands behind my legs and repeatedly taking me down. Whenever we land on the mat I can feel the air leaving my body and with it my desire. I just give in during the scrambles for dominant positions. She submits me over and over. All the fight that was building in me over the last frustrating weeks has been drained away and drowned in alcohol. This exhaustion makes me philosophical. I no longer see the point in resisting: death will have the final word anyway.

If I'd only stopped after three or four drinks last night I'd be fine. Anyway, I wouldn't be incapacitated, so ripe for exhaustion and humiliation. But as the psychologist William James wrote about drinking in *The Varieties of Religious Experience*, "It is part of the deeper mystery and tragedy of life that whiffs and gleams of something that we immediately recognise as excellent should be vouchsafed to so many of us only in the fleeting earlier phases of what in its totality is so degrading a poisoning." Lying on the mat unable to get out of the chokehold of a woman I would have no trouble beating if I weren't always engaged in a war with myself, I understand for the first time this idea of alcohol as poison. And I lash out at myself for falling victim to it again, and on such a joyous occasion as my rebirth.

————

Why do I do this to myself? Why would a perfectly healthy, reasonably intelligent man spend half his life slowly poisoning himself—like the murderer in a detective story slipping polonium or thallium or some other slow-acting killer into his victim's drinks every night at dinner, leaving no trace? Why do I self-destroy through drugs and drink and nicotine and lousy food? Why do I indulge this instinct for self-destruction, for self-loathing, through temporary physical pleasure? Is it an act of philosophical/anthropological rebellion against the realities of my death, a planting of the flag saying, "I refuse to die! I won't die! I can do anything to myself I want!"? Or is it a celebration of the exigencies and variability and variety and internal absurdity of life, of the knowledge that everything occurring is in the process of passing away, like Boethius with his wheel? Is it both? Does the fact that so many of us seek out these approximations of death mean the body has an intuition of its own demise? And is the instinct to drink and eat myself sick the same instinct that motivates me to fight, to put myself in harm's way, to seek out pain in a cage? Is it self-loathing or self-celebration to drink and to fight? Are they mirror reflections of each other: one self-negation through pleasure, the other self-affirmation through suffering? Is it the ultimate act of resignation and acceptance of death to tease it and touch up against it? Or are excessive drinking and cage fighting acts of inoculation against the pain of the knowledge of death? Is that what fighting is: a dress rehearsal for the inevitable? Or is it rebellion against that inevitability?

This is a worthy catechism.

Neuroscience tells us that we drink for pleasure and to conquer social phobias. Ethanol, the psychoactive ingredient in alcohol, activates dopamine neurotransmitters, which help control the brain's reward and pleasure centers. Ethanol also enhances the function of the gamma aminobutyric acid (GABA) neurotransmitter, which regulates levels of fear and anxiety in the brain, allowing people to feel more at ease around each other, reducing inhibition and facilitating social interaction. Ethanol is mankind's social lubricant.

Not entirely satisfied by this scientific explanation, I seek out the comforts of psychology. One therapist tells me we drink to escape the tyranny of the self, to establish, even if only temporarily, something like unmediated connection to the world and to our fellow man. A second believes we drink to control and manage how vulnerable we are to pain and misery and death. A third says we drink simply to avoid anxiety.

All of which rings true but doesn't resonate deeply enough. Of course I drink to calm anxiety and to blot out the awareness of inevitable death, but I'd like to think my drunkenness is bigger than that, more noble and vital, that it's part of a quest for something inscrutable and mysterious and unnameable: that I drink because I'm looking for more life. Under the influence of alcohol the world sparkles and shimmers with a transience and immediacy not available through the sober brain. The overwhelming experience of a good drunk—an abstract, poetic, painter's drunk—wipes out the monotony of the everyday and the terrifying belief that, deep down, life is minuscule in its possibilities. The thrill of the drunken moment is a burst of emotional and aesthetic expansion that allows the damaged mind to believe it has found its way at last to the vast light of perfect knowledge and happiness, and this without the awful slow-moving tyrannical hard labor of actual self-awareness through therapy or the painful vulnerability of establishing emotional connections to other things and commitments to other people. Through alcohol I can remain closed but *appear* open.

William James again: "The sway of alcohol over mankind is unquestionably due to its power to stimulate the mystical faculties of human nature, usually crushed to earth by the cold facts and dry criticisms of the sober hour. Sobriety diminishes, discriminates, and says no; drunkenness expands, unites, and says yes. It is in fact the great exciter of the *yes* function in man. It brings its votary from the chill periphery of things to the radiant core. It makes him for a moment one with truth. . . . The drunken consciousness is one bit of the mystic consciousness." I've never considered my habit in spiritual terms, but I know what James means: drinking provides the potential for glittering experience in a dull world. Jesus was right: in wine lies the glimmering truth.

When I first spoke with the promoter who agreed to put me into a fight a few weeks ago, I was getting drunk inside Jimmy's Corner, a boxing-themed bar located off Times Square in Midtown. Opened in 1971 by James Lee Glenn, a forgettable fighter who came up through the Police Athletic League but who worked his way into the New York State Boxing Hall of Fame as a trainer and cut man, Jimmy's is narrow and dimly lit, every inch of every wall covered in fight posters (Joe Frazier vs. Muhammad Ali, Oscar De La Hoya vs. Ike Quartey) and signed pictures of fighters who have visited over the years, like Mike Tyson and Manny Pacquiao. Now it's a relic from New York's dark and dangerous past, surrounded by its bland and glittering present. I can't remember why I was there getting drunk on a Wednesday afternoon, but looking back it felt like the perfect place to make my intentions to fight official, buoyed by all that history and the pictures of all those fighters and by whiskey and the courage it brings.

After enough heavy use, alcohol eventually hijacks the brain circuitry involved in motivated behavior and natural rewards, the circuitry that tells us to find pleasure in things like food and family and sex and sober life. Ethanol activates dopamine more strongly than those things, and so the brain's wiring pathways adapt to this new stimulant, giving it precedence over other pleasures and slowly coming to need those enhanced levels of dopamine to activate the same feeling of pleasure and reward.

Gradually, as the body becomes used to consistent alcohol use, the circuitry in the brain changes. Determining that there is now too much dopamine and perpetually seeking homeostasis, the brain adapts by down-regulating the amount of the neurotransmitter it's producing. It now requires more alcohol to activate dopamine in levels high enough to provide pleasure, and the dopamine reward volume when there's no alcohol in the body is turned way down. Heavy drinkers start to experience anhedonia, the inability to feel pleasure, when they're sober. Without alcohol life ceases to be stimulating or enjoyable. The glimmer is gone. Sufferers drink now not to get high but merely to feel normal. Some neuroscientists call this the "transition to the dark side."

My desire to fight comes from an instinct and drive for immediate profound experience similar to the one that drives my desire to drink. So one would think the two taken together—opposite sides of a wonderful life-hungry coin—would make for a perfect complement, an ideology of contradictions to build an en-

tire life around: the Philosophy of Drinking and Fighting. The
problem is that as I get closer to my fight and as the demands
that preparations for that fight are putting on my body get more
severe, it's becoming clear that drinking and fighting are actually
incompatible, no matter what the poets, the novelists, or the bar-
stool drunks say. During my early days as a fighter, when training was the end in itself, I could get drunk every night and fight
every morning and not notice any impairment. I wasn't trying to
get anywhere in particular, so what difference did it make if my
advancement was being held back by regular acts of voluntary
self-destruction? Fighting, for all its meaning to me, was just an
abstraction then, just one element of a varied life. There were
no finish lines and nothing specific to strive for, so progress had
no need to be charted, judged, or even acknowledged. But now,
with a real fight out there in front of me, and now that progress
can and will be charted, either in its presence or its lack, there
for all to see when I step into the cage, I can *feel* the effect of my
debasement every time I step into the gym after a night of heavy
drinking. It's as if evolution has gifted humanity with the ability to seek only one heightened experience at a time. Only one
transport can take you to the radiant core. Try them both at
the same time and the true experience of either is lost and your
hopes are dashed. Drinking and Fighting as a life's philosophy is
proving impossible.

This is the irony of fighting: the stronger you get—the more
in shape and skilled and healthy and menacing and intimidating
and capable you are of causing true damage—the more delicate
you become. Your whole system is so finely tuned and calibrated
by that hard work and austerity that it takes almost nothing to
bring it all to a grinding halt.

———

There are neurological similarities between the effects of alcohol and the effects of fighting. Both activate the dopamine system and trigger the release of endorphins, neurochemicals produced in the hypothalamus and pituitary gland that activate opioid receptors in the brain to diminish pain and heighten pleasure. Alcohol, like fighting, also causes the brain to tell the adrenal glands to release adrenaline into the bloodstream, which then transports the hormone to the rest of the body, preparing it for confrontation.

At some point, though, a brain rewired by alcohol is less interested in health than it is in finding rewards. Though what neuroscientists call the reptile brain is controlled by the evolved prefrontal cortex, providing impulse control and feedback to an otherwise irrational and primordial system, chronic alcohol use can damage that feedback system, resulting in less judgment and more self-destructive behavior. The old areas of the brain begin to prioritize the production of dopamine over everything else. In extreme cases the frontal cortex has been shown to physically shrink in response, as if the human is surrendering to the animal.

Now that I'm going to the gym every day and pushing my body much harder than it's ever been pushed before, I feel every indulgence and every sin, every glass of booze and every cigarette. And I feel like those sins are there for all my teammates to see and take advantage of, like they're written on my body. Every straying from the righteous, narrow path is manifested in a lousy round of sparring; every drink can be seen on my flushed face and heard in my gasping breath. Suddenly my self-destructiveness, which always seemed so abstract, so off in the distance, is right there in front of me, making clear just how much damage I've done and am still doing to myself. This is the religious side of training, the punitive side: commit the sin and the punishment comes inevitably.

Still, I believe I can find a way to make this work, that I can simultaneously prepare for a cage fight and drink myself into dissipation. To do this I decide the best approach is to confine my drinking to the weekends. This way I can mold my body and mind into perfect, uncorrupted, fighting form while continuing my search for the mystic consciousness. Dividing up my weeks in this way will allow me to live and celebrate my beloved contradictions, to acknowledge and pay tribute to my warring impulses, to refuse to cut myself off from the full variety of life and the vast expanse of my desires. This won't be a philosophical battle taking place on some airy abstract plane or in the vagueness of the mind or in some book. I want to live the philosophy. I want to celebrate the contradictions. I want to rebel every weekend against the religious tyranny of discipline and purity and self-flagellation and every weekday against the self-destruction and mystical delusion of debasement and dissipation. I want it all.

But every Monday morning at the gym gives the lie to my philosophy, and every sparring session after a long, decadent weekend is more evidence of my unrelenting self-sabotage. What I convinced myself was testament to the limitless capacity of multitudinous personality—proof not only that *I* can be a fighter and a decadent at the same time but that *all* humans in love with life can and should be as well: that the True Philosophy lives!—is really just repeated self-inflicted implosion.

As they age, heavy drinkers begin literally wasting away. They experience an accelerated loss of muscle mass, caused primarily by a decrease in muscle protein or synthesis, which can lead to decreased strength and locomotion. There is also a decrease in the production of the human growth hormone, limiting muscle growth and repair.

After forty, the organs that metabolize alcohol, like the liver and the stomach, shrink, so alcohol stays in the system longer. And since there is less fluid in the body as it gets older, alcohol isn't broken down as quickly in the bloodstream. All of which means the negative physical effects of alcohol abuse, like hangovers, last longer.

After months or years of alcohol abuse, the brain changes its chemical structure to work with a consistent supply of alcohol. The proteins that relay information in the brain are altered, as is the relationship between neurotransmitters and cells and synapses. The entire neurological system exists in some capacity in relation to alcohol and adapts to its constant presence.

When the body is suddenly denied alcohol after years of heavy use, the brain decreases the function of the GABA system, which regulates fear and sedation, and aggravates the amygdala, resulting in moodiness, depression, cognitive dysfunction, paranoia, excitability, tremors, sleep problems, and anxiety. All problems you don't want to be experiencing just weeks before a fight. And all problems that can be solved by giving up quixotic notions and going back to drinking.

Norman Mailer wrote that the monotony of a fighter's life in the depths of a training camp "creates an impatience with one's life and a violence to improve it." After just a few weeks of my new, even more ascetic regimen, this one completely free of alcohol, I know that no truer words have ever been written. All this misery two months before my fight, all this drudgery, all this repetition, all this sobriety, serves a purpose: to conjure up displeasure, create a sense of workaday progress, and demystify the process of becoming a fighter, both the cruelty of it and the fear. It turns something terrible and terrifying into a job, like laying bricks. Which is the whole aim of training for a fight: to cultivate and harness all that misery, all that boredom, and direct it outward, to make your opponent the embodiment of everything you hate, to habituate yourself to fear and pain and anger.

My boredom as I settle into my new sober regimen is all-encompassing. Though I dread the fight, I dread it less than the numbing, soul-deadening repetition of preparing for it. The fight at least would be something different. More fit of body than I've ever been but deep in a black mood brought on by monotony and withdrawal, I'm starting to hate fighting. I hate jogging in circles. I hate jumping jacks. I hate squats, I hate push-ups, I hate heel kicks, I hate high knees, I hate crunches, I hate forward rolls, I hate backward rolls, I hate stretching, I hate judo *gis*, I hate jock-straps, I hate punching, I hate kicking, I hate chokes, I hate getting punched and getting kicked and getting choked, I hate my teammates and my coaches, I hate the smell of the locker room, I hate the feel of the mat under my feet, I hate the heat that blasts through me when I walk into the gym and the humidity that clings to me like misery, I hate walking out into the late-autumn Manhattan cold still dripping sweat from a long session and the wind from off the Hudson River whips right up Thirtieth Street and through my sweatshirt and coat, I hate taking the N train from Brooklyn to Manhattan, I hate taking the train back home, I hate the walk from the train station to the gym past the tourists and businessmen rushing toward Penn Station and the drunken hockey fans stumbling toward Madison Square Garden, past the outdoor café on Thirty-second Street where happy-hour patrons drink and smoke and mock my puritanism every night, I hate the short woman at the top of the station stairs in Manhattan selling the *Daily News* and the teenagers clustered together at the top of the station stairs in Brooklyn refusing to make room for me and my giant heavy bag . . . which I hate. I hate it all with a passionate fury.

On bad days, when this choler clings to me, I can barely drag myself around the gym. I can feel my body and mind rebelling at the thought of warming up—the great refusal of a freeborn man with a mind and soul forced by circumstance to run in endless circles. On days like these even my response to getting punched in the face has less to do with pain or fear than with distaste for its sheer predictability. I drag my feet over the mat and grab onto my partner's neck and upper arms not through any strong desire or power of will or strength of character but out of pure muscle memory and a profound resignation to the deal I've made. I have no more claim to agency or self-propulsion than a spoke in a wheel.

Only now I don't even have the comfort of alcohol to alleviate all the boredom and monotony I've created for myself, to allow my mind some reprieve or even the life-giving joy of a little rebellion. How dull life can get when the monastic, dehumanizing repetition of the gym amplifies the boredom of life without intoxication. And vice versa.

I know I'm sacrificing my life-giving indulgences for a chance at this other kind of rarefied life-giving experience: total self-denial, discipline, purity. But I also know this is an experiment in self-control and abstention that I'll never be able to sustain. Which is why I could never be a real lifelong fighter: not the fear of physical harm but the fear of a life stripped of indulgence, of a life constrained, proscribed, bounded, in denial of all its wonderful and terrible diversity.

But that's a concern for another life. For now I deny myself and I watch what I eat and drink and I run in endless circles, around and around and around, hour after hour, day after miserable day, world without end, building my body at the expense of my soul. This is my *new* philosophy: Trade in one act of self-destruction for another and call it progress.

8

THE GATHERING DARKNESS

(ONE MONTH OUT)

In the time line of the fighter's life, the last month before a fight should be monastic in spirit. To make sure he's walking into a cage prepared for a life-or-death affair, the fighter has to lock himself away and make an enemy of the world and anything that is not *in him*. Traditionally, boxers will disappear from their city homes to upstate rural campsites, finding solace in the boredom and disorientation of the natural world, better to focus their minds and immerse themselves in the long runs and bruising sparring sessions and the thousand and one acts of self-denial that will build up the necessary defenses around them. One reporter writing in the early 1960s described then–heavyweight champion Floyd Patterson's run-down camp in rural Connecticut as "an abandoned road house." While training there Patterson refused to see his wife and children.

Mixed martial artists, too, will go into a shell of self-obsession, not dissimilar from that entered by astronauts who fear falling ill before a mission. Their lives become focused entirely on their gym and their diet and their weight and their routine and their health. Jobs and domestic duties are ignored, friendships and romances cast aside, politics and pressures temporarily forgotten. Fighters come to believe their fight is the entire world. This is an ugly necessity. Without that kind of solipsism and single-minded devotion they'd be putting themselves into a suicidal position. A sense of perspective and proportion would be death to them. The best comparison is a Benedictine laboring away in a monastery. Monks fearful for the state of their souls absent themselves from the world to think on God. Fighters fearful for the state of their bodies absent themselves from the world to think on themselves: *my* technique, *my* pain, *my* struggle, *my* desire, *my* victory, *my* loss. It's a religion of the self.

One month out from my fight, when I should have been retreating into the confines of my own self-obsession, far from the concerns of the world, I found myself not in my MMA gym in Manhattan or my boxing gym in Brooklyn or even in my apartment studying fight footage on YouTube, but ninety miles southwest, wandering the working-class Kensington enclave of North Philadelphia, knocking on strangers' doors. In this neighborhood of shabby row houses and abandoned lots I was hoping to motivate residents—most of them Vietnamese immigrants, Latin Americans, and young white couples—to vote in that day's presidential election and to help hold back the tide of fascism that I felt sure was now beating at the country's door. *Hello, sir, I just wanted to remind you it's Election Day and the world is on the verge of collapse.* The week before, I had foregone too many hours of desperately needed training time to call these same voters (and voters like them in Florida and North Carolina and Arizona) from my apartment in Brooklyn, imploring them to throw their support behind the candidate not endorsed by actual Nazis.

Now, after the heartbreak of Election Night, after which I assumed I would be able to return to the monasticism of my gym and my writing desk, I find myself instead consumed by a new and paralyzing obsession. My sleep is troubled by visions of mobs in the streets and angry racists with shaved heads, my writing time ruined by intimations of mass deportations and American pogroms.

I should be living in the gym. As a natural striker with middling jiujitsu skills, I should be drilling my takedown defense and grappling reversals in order to keep the fight from going to the ground and give myself a chance. There are still many painful, humbling, enlightening hours of work left before me. Instead my days are filled with the damned outside world. All of a sudden there are online petitions to sign and rallies to attend and chants to chant and hopeful political strategies to ponder and arguments to have and Internet news to obsess over. And most of all there is the fear—the anxiety of an American-born Jew long accustomed to the peaceful embrace of his country but also raised from birth to be on the lookout for sudden violent outbursts by the gentile world against his people. Some terrible communal memory is stirring in my blood.

Here, at this most crucial moment, I'm feeling for the first time the meaninglessness of my desires in the face of great historical upheavals. I'm becoming politically awakened at the most inconvenient moment. When I need to be at my most self-obsessed, I'm thinking about my fellow man. Fighting requires unquestioned belief in the seriousness of the enterprise. Doubts and perspective and other abstractions are poison to the fighter's soul, as are outside concerns. Yet here I am, only one month away, drowning in the world and in abstractions.

———

In March 1966, Muhammad Ali declared himself a conscientious objector against the war in Vietnam, citing his religious beliefs and his disdain for the United States government's treatment of African Americans. "Why should they ask me to put on a uniform and go ten thousand miles from home and drop bombs and bullets on brown people in Vietnam while so-called Negro people in Louisville are treated like dogs?" Ali asked one reporter. It's hard to remember now, but opposition to the war was still in its early stages then, and as a minister in the much-reviled Nation of Islam, Ali was still years away from cultural sainthood, which meant his refusal was met with vitriol by much of mainstream white America. He was attacked in the press, both sporting and otherwise, and by politicians and members of the public and even some of his fellow fighters. The legislature in his home state issued a proclamation saying Ali brought "discredit to all loyal Kentuckians and to the names of the thousands who gave their lives for this country during his lifetime." He was put under investigation by J. Edgar Hoover's FBI and faced up to five years' imprisonment for his refusal. Still, somehow, during all that turmoil and sudden infamy, Ali managed to find the time to train for a title defense, a fifteen-round fight at Madison Square Garden in March 1967 against Zora Folley, a stocky Texas native with a big overhand right. It was a fine fight, but Ali, younger than Folley by a decade and much faster, slowly wore down his challenger and, midway through the seventh round, caught him with a beautiful cross-counter right that sent Folley collapsing to the canvas facefirst and unconscious.

A month after the fight Ali refused induction into the military. He was promptly stripped of his title and, after being found guilty of evading the draft, banned from boxing entirely. He wouldn't fight again for three and a half years.

———

As I write, America is entering a dark new period, one where the worst elements in the culture are feeling emboldened and paranoia is spreading to everyone I know. Reports and rumors of harassment and violence against minorities are everywhere in the first weeks after the election. Every day a new threat or swastika is found spray-painted on some wall, and stories about women in hijabs getting harassed and Latin American immigrants getting attacked are common even in liberal New York City. I'm beginning to wonder if these dark forces will make their presence felt at my fight. After all, where better for Nazis to gather than at a cage fight, to get themselves riled up on all that violence and to bark their ridiculous chants from the anonymity of a crowd made rabid by the sight of blood and the swell of testosterone: *Trump! Trump! Trump!* This has always been the risk you run by falling in love with MMA: rubbing shoulders with the uglier side of the American experience, those thugs and goons who adore violence for violence's sake and who seem to revel only in the coarseness and cruelty of fighting, not its art—like British football hooligans who see a soccer game as merely a pretext for a melee. But these unwanted elements always felt like a minor subculture of MMA, a few bad apples tucked away in a corner, drunkenly caterwauling, something you could manage and even ignore. But now who can say, when nothing seems manageable or ignorable? Will they show up at the arena en masse? And if they do, will just the sound of my name being announced arouse ancient hatreds and kick off something horrible in them? Is their loathing for Jews, for African Americans, for Hispanics, for Muslims, for women (who, taken together, will make up at least half the night's fighters) as deep inside them, as inextricable, as unnoticed and unnamed as my terror of that loathing? This is just what I need: fear of the crowd to go along with fear of my opponent.

In 1933 Werner Seelenbinder, a Greco-Roman wrestler of Prussian descent and a devoted member of the German Communist Party, refused to give the Nazi salute when he won a medal at the German wrestling championship. The new fascist government punished the light heavyweight by banning him from training and competing for sixteen months. After the ban Seelenbinder returned to training at the request of the Communists, who recognized that the wrestler's fame and sporting success granted him the rare ability to travel across Germany and to other countries, making him the perfect secret courier for the antifascist resistance.

By the time of the 1936 Olympics in Berlin, Hitler's Olympics, Seelenbinder was not only one of the country's most famous athletes but also a member of the underground anti-Nazi Uhrig Group. He was arguably Germany's best wrestler then, but he was so disgusted by the regime's propaganda machine that he vowed to boycott the Games. Friends convinced him to compete, though, and to use the medal ceremony as a chance to throw up a vulgar gesture in place of the Nazi salute, a small but dangerous act of political resistance in a growing nightmare. But Seelenbinder's plans for civil disobedience were dashed when he came in fourth place and was unable to secure a place on the medal podium. That he got that close under the circumstances was a small miracle.

Seelenbinder continued his work in the Uhrig Group for the next six years after the Games, but on February 4, 1942, he and sixty-five other members of the organization, including its leader, Robert Uhrig, were arrested by the Gestapo. The wrestler was tortured for eight days. He was then shipped to nine different camps and prisons over the next two and a half years before being found guilty of treason by the Volksgerichtschof, the Nazis' "People's Court," which had jurisdiction over what the regime considered crimes that contributed to the "disintegration of defensive capability." Seelenbinder was sentenced to death and on October 24, 1944, he was beheaded with an ax. During his prime the wrestler competed at 198 pounds. When he was killed he weighed 132.

There's another problem now as well, beyond my fear and sudden lack of concentration: historical circumstance is forcing my finely cultivated desires to shift against my will. The cage and its lures are losing their significance, and their pull suddenly seems too small for my ambitions. For years, when I dreamed about using the training and knowledge I'd acquired during all those hours in the gym, the only worthwhile depository for them seemed to be a ring or a cage. I was, after all, a civilized human being, and had no real lust for testing myself in the streets or harming anyone.

But now? What could I care for rings and cages and rules and rituals and aesthetics and communion when there might be real fighting to be done? Fighting in the streets. Against Nazis, no less?! What a nightmare and a dream this is turning out to be for an American Jew. A chance to face his deepest, darkest, most complete fear, and a chance to rewrite history, to correct it through resistance and bravery. This is the kind of fighting that thrilled my soul on countless nights as I drifted off to sleep as a child. In my mind I indulged the cinematic revenge fantasies of every young man who has carried deep in him since birth the knowledge of his people's near extinction. This feels like fighting blessed with perfect nobility. Not to run from Nazis but to destroy them! Not to repeat your people's past but to redeem it! The thrill of a thousand MMA fights couldn't possibly compare with the transcendence of such fear and the casting off of such historical weight.

I can't deny there's a part of me that wants to be on the subway the next time some thug with a Sharpie starts drawing swastikas on the walls and intimidating Muslim women in head scarves, or waiting in the Jewish cemetery when a group of anti-Semites arrive to desecrate the headstones—to flush the Nazis out of New York like Meyer Lansky and his gang of Jewish mobsters busting up German-American Bund rallies in the 1930s with bats and blackjacks. Part of me wants to test myself as a fighter *for real*, without gloves and rules and decency, and at the expense of fascists. Part of me wants to get in touch with those darker spirits residing at the heart of my diversion. Fighting didn't start in a cage with referees. It didn't start with gloves or rounds or cocktail waitresses. Fighting is that other thing— that awful thing inside ourselves that we loathe and lust after in equal measure. After all, this is exactly what Imrich Lichtenfeld designed Krav Maga for: not fitness or fun or weight loss or a shot of endorphins or an improved self-image, but beating back racist gangs in the streets. Suddenly fighting in a cage doesn't seem like enough, where before it seemed like far too much.

That I started my combat education in a Jewish martial art was no accident. I can see that now. That history has seen fit to place this latest rise of fascism outside my window seems like more than mere coincidence, even to my skeptic's soul. That in my more optimistic moods I see this horrible new state of political affairs as an *opportunity*—to put my skills to some good use, to find redemption for my cowardice and for my long-mistreated people through violence, to *live* by beating back those who would darken and destroy life—is undeniable. Shameful but undeniable.

Out there somewhere a man is training every day to harm and humiliate me, unburdened by history, possibly unaffected by the suddenly perilous state of American democracy, maybe even inspired by it. But while he's getting closer to the cage, I feel a thousand miles away from it and from him and weighed down with perspective, worst of all possible fates. The danger is coming from all sides now.

9

WASTING AWAY

(ONE WEEK OUT)

When I made the decision to fight back in January I weighed 195 pounds. Though I'd been training for years by then and had several flirtations with temperance, my body was almost always full of scotch and rich foods and countless other indulgences. I never once sacrificed my desires to the demands of the gym. Today, though, after a solid year of athletic discipline and some professional nutritional advice and a few honest attempts at moderation, I weigh 180. I'm slated to fight as a welterweight, so if I'm not down to 170 by five o'clock Thursday evening, just six days from now, I'll have to forfeit. Which means a fresh new misery has entered my life, the thing I've been dreading most since this fighting idea first floated into my head: cutting weight.

Faced with the prospect of meeting another human being in a cage to exchange blows, fighters will seek out any possible advantage, and there is no advantage like size. The larger a fighter is, the more force he can generate with his punches and kicks, the more torque he can put into his submissions, the more difficult he will be to take down, the more exhausting getting out from under him will be, the more fear he can inspire.

So most mixed martial artists fight in weight classes far below their natural weights. To do this requires a devoted denial of the body's needs and wants for weeks, even months: no sugar, no alcohol, no joy at all. Then, in the week leading up to a fight, fighters will go a step further and drain pounds of water weight from their bodies, literally sucking themselves dry, only to put as much of it back in as they can in the twenty-four hours between weigh-ins and fight time. Which means fighters on the scale often barely resemble the men who walk into the cage a day later. Drained of water and calories, they often look like they're on the brink of death, all ribs and sinew, with dull skin and deep black circles under their eyes. They look more like reminders of mortality than proof of athletic vitality. The next day, as if by magic, they reappear looking like conquerors, born again into all their physical strength and destructive power.

Years ago I met an Ultimate Fighting Championship middleweight fighter during a documentary shoot. Middleweights fight at 185 pounds, and at the time I weighed 195. Yet when I stood next to this man, who was then at his normal "walking-around" weight, I felt like his little brother. He towered over me. His broad chest and shoulders made him appear half again as wide as I was. He seemed to exist at some later marker on the human evolutionary chain. My hand was enveloped in his when we shook. I felt physically insignificant in his presence.

When he was fighting at 205 pounds, former UFC contender Chael Sonnen would walk around at 240. Lightweights Gleison Tibau and Gray Maynard weighed in at 155 pounds for their fights but ballooned up to 185 afterward. Thiago Alves used to cut down from 200 pounds to 170. Before moving up from welterweight to light heavyweight, Anthony "Rumble" Johnson routinely dropped forty pounds from his walking-around weight. He would step onto the scale looking like a ghost and then a day later walk into the cage looking like a linebacker. Former 185-pound champion Anderson Silva walks around near 230. The man who took his belt, Chris Weidman, once cut thirty-four pounds in two weeks.

Before beginning a serious weight cut, wealthy fighters will employ teams of nutritionists, dietitians, and doctors. These experts will analyze their blood for deficiencies and imbalances and to determine the nature of their body composition: What percentage of their weight is fat? What percentage is bone mass? How much of their weight is due to edema, the swelling caused by excess fluid trapped in the body's tissues, and so how much water is there to be drained out?

In what may seem like a counterintuitive approach to weight loss, these fighters will superhydrate their bodies in the weeks leading up to a fight. This approach speaks to the body's eternal quest for homeostasis. By drinking gallons of water a day the fighter trains his body to believe that hydration is never more than thirty minutes or an hour away, no matter how much it's working or sweating in the moment. Which means the body feels no need to panic. It doesn't need to hold on to any excess liquid, so it gladly expels it.

Fighters with fewer financial resources, faced with the prospect of losing fifteen or twenty pounds in a week without expert help, will turn to far more desperate and dangerous methods. Many will cut salt out of their diet entirely, since sodium causes the body to retain water. Some will stop drinking fluids days before their weigh-ins. Others will put themselves through long, exhausting sauna sessions to sweat out as much water as possible. The irony is that this kind of voluntary deprivation, in addition to being perilous and damaging to athletic performance, is counterproductive. Dehydration triggers the body's survival instincts. Habituated into believing no more liquid is coming in, the body will hold on jealously to what it has, expelling nothing and keeping the fighter from losing weight.

In addition to sitting in saunas and denying themselves fluids, some fighters will train in rubberized suits, drain themselves in steam rooms, use diuretics and laxatives, and even force themselves to vomit. In a 2015 study, the California State Athletic Commission determined that 39 percent of mixed martial artists were entering fights dehydrated, which can lead to renal failure, visual impairment, reduced cognitive function, muscle damage, lower cardiac output, hormonal imbalances, heart attacks, and increased risk of brain injury. To say nothing of the drop in performance.

I have no doubt that cutting weight, even done wisely and without any real risk of death, will be the biggest challenge I face in my short fighting life: bigger than trying to master the techniques of five different martial arts, bigger than running hundreds of miles on treadmills and doing thousands of crunches, bigger than dragging myself into a performance in front of hundreds of strangers, bigger even than overcoming my lifelong fear of physical confrontation. While I have, from time to time, out of guilt or a sense of decency or simple boredom, tried to curb my appetites, every attempt I've ever made has ended in failure, never lasting more than a week. Eventually and always my desires have the last word.

But now the days of self-denial and reckoning are finally upon me. Booze is long gone and starches are gone and processed foods are done and I abandoned marijuana weeks ago out of fear of failing a drug test. And today, four days from the fight, I gave up my beloved chocolate, which has been my greatest pleasure since I was a child: my earliest and longest-lasting addiction. I'm now denying myself everything. All the vices my body has come to depend on over the last twenty years, all the emotional crutches my mind has been using to make sense of this world, have been snatched away. I've completely abandoned my devotion to the philosophy of libertinism and self-indulgence. Pleasure has been replaced by discipline and restraint. I've become a shadow of myself, left with nothing but the hope that there's enlightenment to be found in deprivation, that the Buddhists were right all along. For the first time in my life I'm healthy, I'm vital, I'm pure, I'm decent, I'm holy, I'm strong, I'm clean, I'm good at last.

I feel like a traitor.

When the body thinks it's starving, it will lower its metabolic rate in order to burn fewer calories. Bent on survival, the body will store more nutrients and expend less energy, meaning a person could eat less but lose no weight. Fighters looking to cut weight without the risk of lingering depletion, decreased performance, and even serious bodily trauma must therefore become craftsmen with their food intake, studying how long it will take each particular food to become fuel for workouts and then leave their system. As their fight gets closer, fighters will eat more frequent

but smaller meals in order to provide the body with enough calories to work with while at the same time allowing it more
opportunity to digest.

Carbohydrates are often considered the key to athletic performance, and therefore their regulation is the secret to a worthwhile weight cut. It does a fighter no good to make weight only
to have no energy to fight with a day later. Carbohydrates are
stored in the liver and the muscles as glycogen. When the body
needs fuel, that glycogen is converted into glucose, the primary
energy source of the muscular system and the brain, and released
into the bloodstream. Some dietitians and fighters encourage
scaling back on carbohydrates during a weight cut because water
binds to them, making losing weight harder, but in the homeo-
static philosophy of weight cutting, a philosophy based as much
on performance and health as weight loss, water isn't viewed as
an obstacle but as the life-giving force it is, second in importance
only to oxygen. The key isn't to do away with carbohydrates
but to understand their mysteries, and to treat one's body like a
finely tuned machine.

I can't afford a nutritionist, much less a team of them, so in the
days before my fight I have to rely on the advice of an experienced teammate or two and my own research. For three days
I devote myself to a strict and Spartan diet, striking a delicate
balance between carbohydrates, fats, and proteins, distributed
over six small meals throughout the day. Long gone are the red
meats and breads and sweets I crave, replaced by simple meals
filled with lean meats, oats, brown rice, fresh fruits, honey, chia
seeds, hemp seeds, and nut butter.

During this time I eat small meals every three hours, the
better to keep my metabolism up and my weight down. For my

first meal of the day I eat two eggs, a half-cup of grapes, half a banana, and eighteen raw almonds. For my second meal I eat 2.5 ounces of Greek yogurt, half a banana, an ounce and a half of strawberries, an ounce and a half of raspberries, and half a tablespoon of olive oil. For my third meal I'm allowed 3.5 ounces of chicken, two ounces of brown rice, 4.5 ounces of strawberries, yet another half a banana, half a cup of grapes, and some watermelon. My fourth meal is the same as my first, my fifth the same as my second, my sixth the same as my third—a painfully repetitive menu that lulls me into a kind of meditative resignation, broken up only by large glasses of water. Throughout the week I'm hungry all the time and convinced I'm suffering every possible side effect of malnourishment: exhaustion, headaches, confusion, dizziness, heart palpitations, fainting, and crankiness. Such crankiness.

All of which I could accept as a tolerable torture if weight cutting *meant something*, if it served a purpose. But it gets you nowhere and gains you nothing. Your opponent will, just like you, be draining ten to twenty pounds of fluid out of his body in the week before the fight and forcing it back into himself the night before you meet. So the two of you will walk into the cage at the same weight—the weight you both should have been fighting at all along if combat sports didn't thrive on a collective delusion—only now you'll both be exhausted and drained and at your physical and emotional nadir. And *that's* when you'll walk into a cage and fight. In a sport where men and women willingly and repeatedly throw themselves into each other's fists and knees, the only true absurdity is the weight cut.

Fighters are the portraits of health and strength, living proof of just how far the body can go, capable of feats far beyond the comprehension of other humans. They consult doctors and physical therapists and nutritionists and anatomy experts and treat their bodies like laboratories for rational thought. They eat right, they run great distances, they master hundreds of techniques and lift thousands of pounds. They rarely mar their bodies with booze or cigarettes. Then, right at the last and most crucial moment, right when logic and care are most needed, reason and science and self-preservation are all thrown out the window and fighters turn instead to the ancient medicinal delusions of flagellation and purges and the comforts of mad tradition. They do the worst thing they could possibly do to their bodies right when their bodies need them most. It would be like shooting up heroin before running a marathon. How like fighters (those incautious thrill seekers) to seek out medical advice that promises greatness even as it brings death closer. The whole thing smacks of the Middle Ages, of mass hysteria and mass hypnosis and a great religious delusion.

During the eighteenth and nineteenth centuries, before diagnosis and observation had become the scientific standard in the world of medicine, doctors often used the most violent treatments they could come up with to correct imbalances in the so-called four humors (blood, phlegm, yellow bile, and black bile) and jolt the body out of its maladies. These methods included bloodletting, intestinal purging, blistering, vomiting, profuse sweating, even skull drilling. Great believers in treating one pain by causing another, doctors in the Age of Heroic Medicine would cut gashes in healthy tissue and then fill them with foreign objects, often dried peas or beans, in order to produce an infection and distract patients from their original malady. Dr. Benjamin Rush, one of the most infamous proponents of this approach and surely the most sadistic signer of the Declaration of Independence, would burn patients' backs with acid and cut them with knives. He would keep their wounds open for months at a time in order to facilitate "permanent discharge from the neighborhood of the brain." He also used starvation as a treatment method.

And here I am, two hundred years later, a child of the twenty-first century, using starvation as a treatment method, like some melancholic blacksmith consumed with bile. But regardless of my skepticism and my philosophical devotion to rational thinking and the observational principles of modern medicine, I don't really have a choice. The traditions of MMA compel me to engage in heroic bouts of weight cutting in order to survive. They trap me in their absurdity by sheer force of historical inertia and cold anatomical reality. If I choose to take the side of reason and fight at my natural, healthy weight, when I walk into the cage my opponent will weigh ten pounds more than I do, and fighting someone who's that much bigger than you is suicide. It's amazing how much more force can be generated by those ten pounds, how much more impactful they can make a punch or a choke. There are fighters who can offset such dramatic disparities in size with their speed and quickness and talent, but I'm not one of them. I need all the parity I can get. So I concede to superstition and I suffer.

Still, I'd be lying if I said there wasn't part of me that enjoys tinkering with myself like a craftsman in his workshop, going over myself with a magnifying glass, bending the world to my needs. My life has become monastic and self-consumed. I spend hours calculating the nutritional value and caloric content of different foods. I keep close tabs on the amount of water I'm drinking. I avoid friends with suspicious coughs or coloring. I fret over my quality of sleep. I bore my wife with the details of every meal and plague her with my shifting moods and hunger-induced irritability. Her schedule must concede to the demands of mine. I count my sit-ups and push-ups and squats. I gaze at myself in the mirror from every angle.

My once-insignificant shoulders are now round and taut. They curve and dip into thick lines that shoot downward between my biceps and triceps like rivers through a valley. My pectoral muscles are well defined and shoot upward in a W from the bottom of my rib cage to my armpits. My chest is now wide and imposing, perched atop a flat stomach on which, in certain lights and in certain moods, I swear I can make out my abdominal muscles. Bulging veins run from my biceps to my wrists and up my neck from my clavicle bones, which jut out impressively. The *vastus medialis* muscles resting over my knees are prominent. I can even claim to have visible calf muscles, where there were never muscles before.

I've traded the self-indulgence of hedonism for the self-obsession of true discipline. And no one says a thing to me about it. The sin of pride is apparently forgiven when you're about to fight in a cage. In my confinement I've found the strangest kind of freedom: from censure, from criticism, from any judgment at all.

Forced dehydration depletes the body of electrolytes, the minerals—like sodium, potassium, magnesium, and calcium—that affect how much water there is in the body, the acidity of the blood, body temperature, blood pressure, hormone secretion, and muscle function, among other things. Massive fluxes in fluid, like those that happen during a severe weight cut, can throw off the balance of electrolytes in the body.

The kidneys help regulate the body's electrolyte balance, and when there's a massive depletion of fluids followed by a massive influx, the kidneys can become strained and the ratio of electrolytes thrown out of order. Because the cells in the body, in particular those responsible for electrical impulses, depend on a delicate balance of sodium and potassium, when that balance is thrown off by severe dehydration and rehydration, the nerve signal along the cardiac fibers that conducts electrical impulses in the heart can be compromised, resulting in an irregular heartbeat, even cardiac arrest.

Sometimes during acute dehydration, the kidneys will attempt to hold on to the potassium and sodium in the body by excreting different electrolytes instead, such as magnesium. When magnesium levels in the body drop too low, muscle cramps, fatigue, and a decrease in mental function can result. Lose too much sodium, meanwhile, and the brain gets lethargic and less alert. Sodium is also necessary for muscle contraction, including cardiac function. When levels drop, the heart starts palpitating, skipping beats, and cardiac output can plummet. High levels of potassium in the blood can result in renal failure and cardiac arrest. Too much calcium and the muscles can contract too quickly; too much magnesium and muscle speed can slow down dangerously. Soon the whole body is spinning out of control.

Removing fluid from the body and the brain can also make fighters more susceptible to concussions. Dehydration causes the brain to shrink, meaning it may shift around more easily in the skull. A bad shot to the head can cause the brain of a dehydrated fighter to rattle around and bang against the skull even more than normally, making it more vulnerable to traumatic injury and lasting damage.

———

In 2015 Yang Jian Bing, a Chinese flyweight mixed martial artist, collapsed before the weigh-ins at an event in Beijing. The twenty-one-year-old died a day later as a result of a dehydration-induced heart attack. Two years earlier Brazilian flyweight Leandro Souza died in the sauna as he was attempting to sweat out two more pounds before a fight. He had been attempting to lose thirty-three pounds, or 20 percent of his body mass, in seven days.

Christ, why am I doing this? What am I risking my heart and my kidneys and my brain for? Why, in the twenty-first century, deep into what I'd always assumed was an Age of *Rational* Medicine, are fighters still cutting weight, starving, and draining themselves in the search for an advantage that isn't there? And why are athletic commissions and fight promotions still letting them? Occasionally a state governing body will respond to a story about some poor depleted fighter having to be rushed to the hospital by making cosmetic changes to their weight-cutting rules—scheduling earlier weigh-ins so fighters have more time to rehydrate, say, or increasing the number of weight classes, or instituting heavier fines for missing weight, or even attempting to force fighters to fight at weights that fall within a certain percentage of their optimum capacity—but the lie itself never goes anywhere. The culture of fighting is built around the delusion that a small size advantage justifies self-marring behavior and the belief that making weight is as difficult, and therefore as noble, as fighting itself. A fighter who misses weight is mocked by his colleagues in a way a fighter who loses a fight never is. Is this some kind of collective psychosis? Is it the thrill of courting death? Is it machismo run mad? Or is weight cutting just more proof of the comforting power of humanity's superstitions and traditions even in the face of overwhelming scientific evidence, even in our Age of Reason?

A few months ago I was sparring in Brooklyn when a member of the staff came up to the ring and told us that the gym's policy prohibited sparring without headgear. Leaving aside the fact that none of us had ever heard of such a policy, had never been prevented from sparring before, and had never seen anyone wearing headgear in the gym, only two weeks earlier the International Olympic Committee had voted to do away with headgear in that year's men's boxing competition in Brazil.

The IOC had started requiring headgear in Olympic boxing competitions thirty years earlier, at the 1984 Games in Los Angeles, in response to a series of articles published in the *Journal of the American Medical Association* the year before calling for a total ban of the sport. The year 1982 had been a dark one for boxing, culminating in the death of South Korean lightweight Kim Duk-Koo in November after a brutal championship fight with Ray "Boom Boom" Mancini, and doctors found themselves running out of ways to rationalize the existence of a sport whose goal seemed to be human misery. So they turned on it. In response, the IOC instituted a headgear requirement in an attempt to "humanize" a sport in peril and make it seem like something was being done to protect fighters—this despite a lack of evidence that there was any medical benefit to wearing headgear in the ring.

Thirty years, seven summer Olympics, and thousands of amateur boxing matches later, studies were released proving what fighters knew all along: that headgear causes extra jarring to their heads, gives them a false sense of security, and impairs peripheral vision, all of which can *increase* the chances of brain

damage. So the IOC did away with headgear at last. Two weeks
after that victory for science and rational thinking, my gym-
mates and I were being told we needed to wear headgear while
sparring "for our safety." Yet another fighting illusion that refuses to die.

Sigmund Freud once described religious beliefs as illusions "de-
rived from human wishes." The same could be said of many of
our most cherished fighting traditions, which have been around
so long and existed in such enthusiastic indifference to rational
thought that they've taken on the air of religious dogma.

Take sex, the great bugbear of the fighting spirit: a spec-
tral, mystical force rumored to drain the fighter of all his powers of destruction, a female demon, a monster of the night, a
seductress, a succubus extracting the lifeblood from men as they
sleep, beckoning fighters from the straight and narrow (the decent, disciplined, noble, violent life of men) to decadence and
collapse, leaving them feminized by delight and pleasure and at
the mercy of their opponents. In the mind of the fighter, sex can
wipe out in one night the work of hundreds of days; it's an act
of self-sabotage and proof of moral weakness. Convinced that
their power lies in their loins and that sexual pleasure drowns
the anger and aggression needed to fight well, fighters have been
abstaining from sex before battle since at least the time of the
Spartans, and by this point the belief in the debilitating power
of sex and the ennobling power of its avoidance is such a fundamental part of the mythology of fighting that it refuses to die, so
potent is its metaphorical power.

Sex is Delilah chopping off Samson's hair, and the Sirens
singing to Odysseus, and Lilith, the "Lady Flying in Darkness,"
seducing Adam in the Garden of Eden and having her way with

men as they sleep. Sex is Circe changing men into pigs and "La Belle Dame Sans Merci" holding kings and princes and death-pale warriors in thrall. Sex is the sinister women of the fifteenth-century witch-hunting manual *Malleus Maleficarum* stealing the genitals off men's bodies by magic and keeping them like pets, shutting "them up together in a birds' nest or some box, where they move about like living members, eating oats or other feed." Sex is the ancient, lingering belief in the life-draining power of the woman over the man. "All witchcraft comes from carnal lust," the author of the *Malleus Maleficarum*, Heinrich Kramer, wrote, "which in women is insatiable."

Boxers in Ancient Greece practiced sexual abstinence and extreme self-control, believing sperm was a source of masculinity and strength and not to be tossed away frivolously. Before fights, a boxer would tie up the foreskin of his penis with a small piece of string called a *kynodesme* to prove his restraint. Kleitomachos, a Theban fighter who won the boxing competition at the 216 and 212 BCE Olympic Games, was famous for his devotion to asceticism and sexual abstinence. Legend has it that he would refuse to participate in conversations about sex and even turned his head away when he saw dogs mating.

    Kynodesme is the Greek word for a dog's leash.

But science tells us that sex doesn't actually drain fighters of testosterone. Sex *stimulates* testosterone production. And higher testosterone levels increase aggression and desire. They also increase muscle production. There is, in fact, no proof that having sex would decrease a fighter's ability to fight, no evidence that having sex decreases testosterone (that aggression can be drained away by the act of love), and no reason to believe that there's only so much testosterone the body can produce and maintain at any given time before it runs out. In a study published in *Frontiers of Physiology* in June 2016, researchers said there "is no robust scientific evidence to indicate that sexual activity has a negative effect upon athletic results." In fact, researcher Laura Stefani said, "unless it takes place less than two hours before, the evidence actually suggests sexual activity may have a beneficial effect on sports performance." Sex, it turns out, can actually *help* a fighter. But the old American puritanism, if dead elsewhere, is still alive in fighting. Like early Christians, fighters are taught to "chastise" their body "and bring it into subjection," to "put to death what is earthly" in them—"For if you live according to the flesh you will die, but if by the Spirit you put to death the deeds of the body you will live." And like believers searching for meaning beyond the "truths" of the material world, we listen, the blind acolytes of an undying myth.

Still, maybe I've been looking at things too literally, too scientifically, and failing to see the metaphysical value in a fighter's forced deprivation. Now that I'm two days out from my fight and starving to death, I'm beginning to see the value in some of these delusions. The longer I go without eating, without drinking, without any of the delights that sustain me, the more acquainted I seem to get with the violence that I've been tucking away and covering up my entire life.

True, there may be no physical advantage to cutting weight and no chemical advantage to abstaining from passion, but it's not hard to imagine how refraining from sex and beloved foods could tamp down the tenderness in a person's soul, making him cold and cruel, fueling his anger and giving him a reason to hate the person he's fighting. Maybe there's another kind of science at play here, something older, something alchemical and mythic

and transubstantial, something out of a late-nineteenth-century
Gothic novel like *The Strange Case of Dr. Jekyll and Mr. Hyde* or
The Island of Dr. Moreau: the science of turning a human being
into something other, something different, something crueler,
something less than, more than, not, sub-, superhuman—like
turning a wafer into flesh and a glass of wine into redemptive
blood. Perhaps the best way to transform a human being into a
fighter is through deprivation.

"From the beginning of the London prize ring, professors
of prizefighting have taught that unremitting exercise, austere
surroundings, and general abstinence to the point of ill temper
constitute the indispensible preparation for combat," the great
boxing writer A. J. Liebling wrote. "Training methods are not
only a conditioning process but a form of torture, designed to
put iron in the soul and to spoil the temper."

It's hard to know before I fight if my abstinence and austerity have put iron in my soul, but I do know they've turned my
temper blacker than it's ever been. My hunger and thirst have
made me angry and bitter and jealous of the life I had before and
covetous and resentful and aggressive and livid and rude and
barbarous and uncivilized and—*I see it now!*—enraged with
the man who has stolen the pleasure from my life. He has become the cause of all my discontent and so must be punished.
Despite all my technical progress over the last year, I was never
sure where the rage necessary to harm another human being in
public was going to come from, but now I can see it and feel it.
Like Mr. Hyde himself, my rage is rising up within me to take
me over, distorting me and making me capable of terrible things.
The denial of the pleasures of the senses makes one cruel in one's
desire for them.

So perhaps the traditions and illusions are right, even if they
aren't medically true: maybe it takes rituals of deprivation to

convert technique and skill and training into rage and cruelty, to take fighting out of the realm of the cerebral and the technical and the athletic and to tap a fighter into his primordial impulses and strip away his civilizing skin. Maybe that's how you transform a human being into a fighter. When it comes to summoning darkness, there's nothing like the old ways.

Without these acts of self-denial I'd remain plagued by my geniality and decency, even a sense of shared humanity, which is death to a fighter. Deny yourself food and booze and water and love and tenderness and lust and all the things that make you human and you become both a beast overcome with rage when denied its physical needs and a spiritual being floating on some higher plane—like a monk free of material desires, born again through suffering. Atavism and enlightenment all at once.

Which makes weight cutting a ritual in the truest and oldest sense, a means of crossing over from one state to another. There may be meaning to my misery after all.

On the day of the weigh-in I consume nothing at all. Not a handful of almonds, not a single egg or slice of unsalted chicken, not a piece of fruit, not even a small glass of water. Every ounce counts now, so you live that day depleted and drained.

My bathroom scale says I weigh 169 pounds, one below the limit, but I have no reason to trust it. And since the idea of not making weight is too horrible to bear, especially in front of all those other fighters, I put on a sweatsuit and wool cap and, despite my fragile state, I run on the treadmill for twenty minutes, somehow wringing from my dehydrated body a few last drips of sweat.

As soon as I make weight I'll begin the process of rehydrating and reintroducing food into my system, which is its own delicate anatomical balancing act. As part of the digestive process the body moves food through the bloodstream, but because of the lack of fluid in my system my blood is now running thick, slowing my ability to absorb nutrients. So I'll have to get fluids back into my body to thin out my blood before I can start eating. But I can't drink too quickly because my body currently doesn't have enough sodium to properly retain water, and too much water introduced into a body low on sodium can trigger hyponatremia, swelling the body's cells. Symptoms of hyponatremia include nausea, confusion, and fatigue. In extreme cases, rehydration-induced electrolyte imbalances can lead to heart attacks, brain swelling, and even death. My nutritional obsessiveness isn't over yet.

For now, though, there's nothing more I can do. I officially weigh less than I have in fifteen years. I'm mean and miserable and weak. I'm the very portrait of fragility. But with any luck, twenty-four hours from now I'll reappear full of fluids and nutrients and electrolytes and blood and muscle and all the things that make up life. Back to my old self, only better, and worse. Lazarus reborn into a life of brutality, with new knowledge. I'll be at my fighting weight with a newfound sense of violence in me, something I can rely on when I get into the cage and fear and adrenaline inevitably conspire against my technique and knowledge and calm. Rescued from a dark tomb and pushed out into the flashing lights of the Space in Westbury, Long Island, I'll be reborn, even (dare I say it?) resurrected. Which is what I've been searching for from the moment I started fighting all those years ago. Rebirth. Renewal. A new life. A new me. Self-creation through self-destruction. Behold the fighter.

10

THE LONG WALK

(TWO HOURS OUT)

Over the course of the day my small dressing room has been slowly filling up with people until there's no room to move and barely enough room to sit. At the very moment when I most need quiet and calm and air and space, I'm surrounded by strangers and crammed into a corner, my gym bag for a footstool. According to the sign hung on the door there are nine fighters assigned to this room (fifteen fights are scheduled for the night), which would already be straining comfort, but when you add in all the coaches and trainers and teammates and other seconds each fighter has, and the numerous officials from the state athletic commission poking their heads in to check on the quality of our hand wraps and the exact spelling of our last names and to make sure we understand the subtleties of this rule or that, the room soon becomes suffocating. All I want is the communion of a little solitude so I can properly contemplate the decisions I've made that got me to this point. And after that maybe some time alone with my coach, Thiago, who will be the only person with me in my corner tonight, to quietly discuss the subtleties of our fight strategy. Instead I'm stuck in a tiny closet of a room with ten, then fifteen, then twenty, then thirty strangers, many of whom, consumed with their own anxiety, won't stop talking. Like the coach from South Carolina, who, I hear over and over, drove up that morning with his team, leaving at 4 A.M. to make it to Long Island in time, and that explains why his fighters are curled up in chairs with jackets over their heads, trying to sleep. Or the fighter from Queens shooting solemn prefight videos of himself on his phone to post online. Or the local Long Island trainer holding court in the corner on the absurdity, even the amorality, of some rule, making sure everyone hears him. "It doesn't make any sense. One minute they're telling us the fight will be over if the doctor comes in the cage, the next they're saying the referee can ask the doctor to come into the cage at any time to consult on an injury, and the referee will decide if the fight goes on from there. Which *rule* are we supposed to believe? It reminds me of the fights I went to in . . ." I tolerate them as long as I can before I get up to wander the hallways for the tenth time since I arrived at the venue.

I drove out too early, that's clear now. But the thought of adding the stress of Friday afternoon New York traffic to the stress of fighting was too much to bear. Every street and every highway would have been miserable if I'd waited until the afternoon to leave: Fourth Avenue and the Prospect Expressway, from there to Atlantic Avenue and Eastern Parkway and then the Jackie Robinson Expressway, which took me out of Brooklyn and into Queens, where my grandparents lived when I was growing up. Near Kew Gardens I merged onto the Grand Central Parkway and took the Northern State Parkway to exit 32, into Westbury, a village of fifteen thousand northwest of Levittown, just now covered in Christmas decorations. I didn't hit traffic anywhere. I'd been told to give myself four hours on a Friday. The entire trip took me an hour and a half, leaving me with six hours to kill once I arrived—six hours to sit and wait and pace and burn and die with anticipation, with nothing to do but think about the cage and the crowd and my opponent, Jon Potts.

Strange what Jon said to his coach in front of me when I drove out to the venue yesterday for the weigh-ins: "That was the easiest weight cut I've had since I wrestled in college." Giving something away, wasn't he? Now I know he's a wrestler. And he doesn't know anything about me. Or maybe he was trying to get one over on me: make me *think* he's a wrestler so I'll prepare to fight a wrestler, then when he finally gets me into the cage it turns out he's not a wrestler at all but a boxer or a Muay Thai specialist. A devious strategy. Or was I being paranoid? I wondered the same thing twenty minutes later, when the referee was explaining the rules and Jon was asking all those questions about the legality of particular grappling techniques. *Can I use my forearm to crossface on the ground? Can I knee him in the body when I've got him clinched against the cage?* Was he really exposing his game plan like that, or was he playing a game with me? Was he trying to intimidate me, or is he just the kind of person who asks a lot of questions when he's nervous? If it was all an act of psychological warfare, I was too hungry then to parse its subtleties.

I didn't eat or drink all day yesterday. That may have been the first time I've ever done that. When I finally got on the scale at the weigh-in and the official said I weighed 169.3 pounds, I wanted to jump off and hug him. It was as if a great burden had been lifted from my shoulders. I could tolerate losing, but telling my friends and my coaches that my fight was canceled because I'd come in overweight would have been too much. Making weight felt like the last barrier between everyday life and the life of a fighter. I'd crossed over. How miserable we all must have looked: thirty hungry, nervous people sitting on a cold stage in an otherwise empty venue waiting to strip down and get weighed in front of a roomful of strangers. There was a real air of quiet and doom about the place, like we were convicts waiting to be led out to the gallows. One flyweight came in four pounds overweight. "You've got a lot of jogging to do," the official told him and pointed to the door. You could actually feel the collective sympathy for him in the room. How was he going to sweat off any more weight in that cold? It was twenty-two degrees outside. How awful: extending the misery and self-denial of the weight cut even longer, and this time in public. Then there were the heavyweights, who didn't have a care in the world. They could weigh anywhere between 205 and 265 pounds, so their weigh-ins were purely ceremonial, and totally devoid of suspense. One of them didn't even take his clothes off. He just took his wallet and phone and keys out of his jeans pockets like he was walking through airport security and still made weight by thirty pounds. I bet he didn't have to change his diet at all, never turned down a drink or concerned himself with caloric content or electrolyte balances. And so the rest of us, gaunt and pale with barely a drop of water in our systems, stared at him with murder in our eyes.

I just learned that Jon Potts's nickname is "The Poet." Yet another writing fighter. Or fighting writer. One of his poems begins, "The wind swept across sheering dunes of white sand / the way certain kinds of dancers sway / like flames / The way young children often play / free of their father's shame." My father is dead ten years now, almost to the day. Would passive, peaceful, cerebral Joel Rosenblatt—who was *consumed* by shame and saved his violence only for himself—would that lover of literature and music have seen the art in what I'm attempting? Would he—whose every third thought, like Prospero's, was his grave—have seen the beauty in confronting death and the humor in teasing the forces of bodily destruction in the name of spiritual equanimity, or would he have recoiled in horror? Would he have been ashamed to learn he'd raised his only son to do *this*? It depends on how sour his mood was.

Fight shorts, saline solution, hand wraps, mouth guard, water bottle, jockstrap, protective cup, change of clothes, extra pair of contacts, nasal spray, shin pads, gloves, earbuds, phone charger, pad and pen, medical forms, but no food. I packed several small meals in my gym bag before I drove out this morning, but now I'm realizing I'm one short. I'm not particularly hungry, but the last thing I want is to lose my fight because I don't have any energy. I'll have to go out for something. The problem is that this is small-town Long Island, not Brooklyn, and I'm under strict nutritional orders. I'm a delicately calibrated machine made of proteins, fats, and complex carbohydrates set to synchronize perfectly in two hours. The wrong food could throw off the entire system, and all I saw on the town's main street when I drove in was the wrong food: Chinese takeout places, fast-food restaurants, a Mexican bar, a kebab house, a 7-Eleven, and a red-sauce Italian restaurant that would, in the delicate state I'm in, lay me out for a week. Still, I need to find something. I grab my coat and head for the door.

As I wander through the quiet frozen streets of Westbury, the wind whipping at my lean body through my coat and sweatshirt, I try to remember what I've read recently about fear and the ways it can be controlled, hoping to find some small advantage. I recall that passivity leads to panic, so the more active you are in a stressful situation, the less anxiety it provokes: action, even ineffectual action, can stave off paralysis and trauma. Yelling and deep breathing can diminish the effects of stress. Fear exists completely in the brain, therefore consciously changing the way the brain assesses a threatening situation can be enough to diminish the fear it causes. The simple act of naming a fear activates the prefrontal cortex and subdues the amygdala, allowing us to regain some control of our response. Social stress (like that experienced when fighting half-naked in front of a roomful of strangers) can override even the most habitual and practiced motor patterns: the fear of humiliation can do away with years of training and muscle memory.

Predictably, I arrive back at the arena empty-handed (I'll have to make do with nuts and fruit). Before I go inside I look up at the old marquee, a remnant from the days when the Space was a single-screen movie house. TONIGHT: LIVE MIXED MARTIAL ARTS. NEXT WEEK: KISS TRIBUTE BAND. The opening-night movie, on November 10, 1927, was *Hula*, starring Clara Bow, who was the greatest sex symbol of her era. Bow had grown up a tomboy, however, in the impoverished Prospect Heights neighborhood of Brooklyn (just around the corner from my current apartment), with no money and few friends, shunned by the girls for her shabby clothes and hair and treated like a boy by the local gangs. "I had one little playmate, though, to whom I was devoted," Bow told *Photoplay Magazine* in a 1928 profile. "He was a little boy who lived in the same house with me. I think his name was Johnny. He was several years younger than I was and I used to take him to school with me, and fight the boys if they bothered him. I could lick any boy my size. My right was quite famous." Even Clara Bow fought.

I walk through the front door of the theater and pass into the main room, blowing into my hands to get them warm again. Everything is now buzzing with noise and activity. Burly event staffers are driving the final screws into the cage and testing the big metal latch on the door, its cold *clank* ringing in my ears, reminding me what I've gotten myself into. Other workers are on high ladders hanging banners for the local tattoo-removal studios, janitorial supply companies, auto-repair shops, and chicken wing restaurants sponsoring tonight's event. I look above them and see men adjusting spotlights from the catwalk. Between the sound of electric screwdrivers and the DJ testing his massive sound system and the clanking of that damn cage door, these men have to shout to be heard by their colleagues down below. The noise in here is overwhelming. I turn around and see hundreds of empty seats that will soon be filled with drunken fight fans crying out for blood, *my* blood. I need to get out of here. I hurry back down the stairs into the quiet basement to catch my breath. When I get there I see Jon standing by himself in the hallway. He looks deep in thought. I walk past him and we don't look at each other or say anything. We just act as if the other person isn't there, as if we aren't about to fight each other in a cage.

The dressing room is much more tense than it was before. This must be how the Roman gladiators felt, packed into a tiny space in the basement of some arena on the outskirts of the empire, fighting off boredom and fear while waiting to die. To distract ourselves we engage in all kinds of ministrations and self-hypnosis. We listen to music and shadowbox and try to sleep. Some fighters trim their nails; others braid their hair. The fight doctors make us do deep squats to make sure our knees aren't damaged and take deep breaths to make sure our ribs aren't broken and we don't have pneumonia. They take our blood pressure. Officials wander from dressing room to dressing room, making sure our hands are wrapped according to the specifications of the state athletic commission, that we're wearing cups and have mouth guards. They fit us for gloves and shin guards.

Ancient Greek boxers wore straps around their knuckles to protect their hands, made of hard leather and wool. Starting in the fourth century BCE, fighters started using gloves with ox-hide straps around the fingers and fur trims they could use to wipe the blood and sweat from their faces. Later, during the Roman Imperial period, when things got serious, gloves were turned into deadly weapons, equipped with sharp metal, lead, iron plates, and broken glass. The Romans called these gloves *cesti*, from the Latin word for "to strike." In his 1697 translation of Virgil's *Aeneid*, the English poet John Dryden translated the word as "gloves of death."

The medical exam is just a formality, really. We've all had to get full physicals done. Three weeks ago my doctor assured me that I was free of HIV and hepatitis B and C, cataracts, chest pains, convulsions, frequent headaches, and visceromegaly, which is an enlargement of the abdominal organs, including the liver, the spleen, and the kidneys. My upper extremities, including my elbows and shoulder girdle, were in fine shape, as were my tendon reflexes, including the Romberg and the Babinski, which is tested by running a pointed object along the plantar surface of the foot laterally from back to front, and which can be indicative of disorders of the central nervous system. My electrocardiogram, a test to check for problems with the electrical activity of the heart, also came back fine. Despite my years of smoking and decades of heavy drinking, I was deemed fit and my body ready to face its destruction.

A man dies alone in a small apartment in some lifeless suburban complex, the way he lived. And by vanishing all of a sudden he leaves his son, then only thirty, perpetually unresolved. Did his son mourn him adequately when he died or had he let go of him years before his actual physical departure? Is his mourning therefore "incomplete," as the therapists say—without catharsis or grief, leaving him with the burden of rage and guilt and sorrow that then become the seeds of self-destruction?

Was the father's death a tragedy, or was he better off gone? And where does it leave his son now, pondering the ineffable and inscrutable, looking everywhere for metaphors and coincidences, never sure if everything he does is an inheritance from his father or an act of rebellion against becoming him? The man who loved books more than anything left a legacy too literary for even his writer son, who now seeks out peace and solace and quiet of mind in violence, the thing his father never touched. This American father and his damn ghost, showing up at the most inopportune times, an abstraction that can't be fought.

All the fighters and their cornermen have gathered in my dressing room to hear the referee go over the rules one last time, which means the room is now filled far beyond capacity. According to the laws of the State of New York, as amateurs we won't be allowed to punch each other in the head on the ground, knee each other in the head ever, or throw any elbow strikes. We'll also be wearing shin guards, whose value will be talismanic at best. Anyone who's sparred knows that shin guards won't prevent a head kick knockout or the sudden paralysis that comes from a perfect shot to the liver. The best they can do is provide a protective psychological blanket that allows a fighter to convince himself he's just in another sparring match at his gym with a gentle and sympathetic partner, not fighting a stranger with real violence in him in front of eight hundred people far from home. These amateur rules are in addition to the professional regulations laid out in the unified rules of mixed martial arts, adopted in April 2001, that prohibit fighters from head butting, eye gouging, hair pulling, fishhooking, biting, spitting, attacking the groin, inserting a finger into an orifice or laceration, manipulating small joints, striking downward with the point of the elbow, striking the spine or the back of the head, kicking the kidney with the heel, striking or grabbing the throat, clawing or twisting the flesh, grabbing the clavicle, kicking or kneeing the head of a downed opponent, stomping a grounded opponent, holding the fence, holding an opponent's shorts or gloves, using abusive language, engaging in unsportsmanlike conduct, attacking an opponent during a break or after the bell has sounded, throwing an opponent out of the ring or cage, spiking an opponent's head or neck, engaging in acts of timidity (including faking an injury), or applying any foreign substance to their hair or body "to gain an advantage." What a bizarre wrestling match humanity is in with itself: inching its way toward civilization while continuing to indulge its worst primordial instincts, like cage fighting. We know intuitively that those instincts are inescapable, that they're too deeply rooted in us to ever get rid of entirely, so instead of snuffing them out, we regulate them, attach rules to them, come up with an aesthetic to judge them, pacify them, quantify them, refine them, alter them, distort them, clean them up, and suck the blood out of them. But the blood is proof of life; the viscerality of these dark instincts *is* their vitality. The rules and regulations we come up with are just the delusion we agree upon, the proof we point to of our evolution from the monstrous to the moral. Which makes sport fighting both an act of unfiltered honesty and the highest form of self-deception.

My own hopes as a fighter parallel this evolution—only in reverse. My desire is to *indulge* my uncivilized self, not to subdue him. What I want most from tonight is the opportunity to forget about my moral self for a while and to tap into the animalistic abandon, the precivilized menace, the monster that is my inheritance.

It's seven o'clock now, just one hour from the start of the event, and I'm still having trouble imagining hitting someone out of anger. This is my last psychological hurdle and the only thing that really worries me now. I can handle losing, but not fighting back would be torture. Once the fight starts, will I become that other person I've only ever imagined I'm capable of being, or deep down am I too inveterate a pacifist and too terrified of the physical and moral consequences of violence to give myself over to it? At the moment I can't say with any confidence. What I'm hoping is that things will become clear in the moment of crisis. Many mixed martial artists claim they don't feel like they're really *in* a fight until they've been hit and made to bleed. The sight of their own blood is a muse, they say, the shock that motivates them. Their instincts toward self-preservation, made dull by years of sparring, of simulated death, don't come alive until the threat of *actual* death, symbolized by the loss of blood, becomes real. Only then does the switch go on in their brain that awakens and gives free license to their animal selves. Maybe this is what I need in order for this abstraction I've been living with for nearly a decade to become concrete: to be hit, to feel truly threatened, to be in pain and desperate, to bleed. Only then, perhaps, will I do away with all the decency and delicacy I've perfected over an entire life and give in to my rage. Let's hope so.

With twenty minutes to go before the fight, Thiago takes me out into the hallway to warm up. As I shadowbox he keeps looking down the hall, where Jon Potts is getting ready with his coach. I can hear the thwack of his gloves against the mitts echoing off the walls. *He looks nervous,* Thiago tells me. *He's moving around too much. He's jittery, too full of energy, like he's going to burst. He's going to attack you early but then he's going to get tired quickly, and you can take him. Just keep throwing your jab and you can take him.* It's just what Thiago and Dorrius have told me dozens of times before. It's just like I've pictured it a million times in my head over the past month, in my apartment, in the subway, while I was writing, while I was cooking dinner, while I should have been paying attention to my wife and friends. All this time I've had that image in my head: Jon rushing in, me staying calm, Jon getting tired, me turning the tables, Jon fading, me victorious.

My wife and friends are probably upstairs by now, handing over their tickets, looking for their seats, taking off their coats, worrying about me, numbing their dread with alcohol, trying to come to terms with this ridiculous psychological predicament I've dragged them into. My mother was supposed to be here, too, but a week ago she decided it was too much to watch her only son fighting, so she didn't make the trip. And who can blame her? What son does this to a mother, what husband to a wife? For the first time this idea of mine—always risky and ridiculous—seems selfish. Pacing the dark hall in a pair of six-ounce gloves and little else, waiting to fight a man who's pacing not ten feet away from me, with my wife and other loved ones right upstairs, dying inside, and my mother at home, dying inside, I can see for the first time that what I'm presenting them with is an impossible dilemma: *Come watch someone you love risk his life! Choose between his safety and his happiness! Love me, love my self-destruction.*

When Jon's coach comes over to wish me luck, I watch Thiago's face, always so sweet and decent, distort into a mask of contempt. It's like some dark force has entered his body to seal us off from the rest of the world. For the first time in my life I feel what it must be like to be in a gang. Thiago is on my team and everyone else is outside that team and therefore is our enemy. That's one way to trip the violence switch in the brain: to create an other out of the man you're fighting, to make an enemy out of a perfect stranger. Thiago might be on to something here. Watching him build a wall around us, I'm so touched I could cry.

Ten minutes now and something I read years ago comes back to me: "Those who are led off to execution—no doubt their thoughts fasten on anything." I can see now how true that sentiment is. My brain is careening from thought to thought as the fight gets closer, grabbing on to anything so it doesn't have to face the grim impending reality. Two of the twelve recessed lights in the hallway are out. The promoters provided us with a huge bin full of Goldfish crackers but no bottled water. I recognize the ring announcer from Muay Thai fights in the Financial District. There are framed autographed T-shirts of bands that have performed here lining the walls between dressing rooms. I first heard Modest Mouse in Tokyo when I was twenty-five, living in an apartment next to a graveyard.

It's eight fifteen. They'll be calling my name any minute now. Thiago tells me I need some kind of spiritual focus, some kind of mantra, some context for this madness, something for my brain to grab on to to keep from spinning out of control. Only the Book of Job comes to mind: "For that which I greatly feared is come upon me, and that which I was afraid of is come unto me. I was not in safety, neither had I rest, neither was I quiet; yet trouble came."

"Josh Rosenblatt! You're up!"

Might as well. I drove all this way.

11

THE FIGHT

Throughout this past year, the only thing I felt truly confident of was that once I finally entered the cage I would be consumed by fear. That much seemed certain. Despite all my years in the gym, there was simply no precedent in my life for such an encounter, nothing that could have prepared me for the experience of walking into a cage to fight another human being. Writers like to believe that we share some psychological sympathy with fighters, a solitary, combative worldview, but at some point, at the *critical* point, the similarities end. So, by the time fight night arrived, I had so thoroughly resigned myself to the likelihood of panic that no reaction would have surprised me. Not if I had curled up in a ball, not if I'd started throwing punches in an artless frenzy, not even if I'd run screaming through the cage door, out of the arena, and down the frozen streets of Westbury, out into the night, never to be heard from again: MMA's vanished soul, the sport's first spook story. On cold nights you can still hear him weeping.

But I couldn't have been more wrong. When the time finally came, fear was nowhere to be found, and in its place was an overwhelming sense of calm, a beautiful resignation to my predicament. It was as if the moment I walked into that cage and looked out at that crowd and felt those lights in my eyes, all my fear and insecurity and even my desire for self-preservation vanished. Like a Buddhist aspirant deep into a life of meditation, I felt a profound, even religious sense of detachment and indifference to material trifles like outcome or consequence or even survival. Winning and losing, even physical suffering, felt like concerns for other people. Maybe I sensed that fear at this late hour wouldn't do me any good. Maybe I'd been waiting so long for this day to come that it was a relief when it finally did, no matter the result. Maybe my devotion to sustaining life wasn't as rabid as I always assumed. Or maybe my fear had metastasized into something much subtler and more sinister, some kind of pretraumatic disassociation I wasn't familiar with, manifesting itself as emotional serenity first, with physical paralysis soon to follow. I had no idea.

Jon Potts had been bouncing around incessantly in the hallway backstage—proof, my trainer told me, of his *lack* of calm— and now that we were facing each other across the cage he was still at it, leaping from side to side on the balls of his feet and shaking out his arms, as fighters do. Meanwhile, I was impassive. My hands were on my hips and I had a blasé look on my face. I could have passed for indifferent. And while I took this as evidence of his anxiety and my early advantage, I also worried that I wasn't performing my assigned role in the traditional prefight rituals, which are, in their way, just as important as the fight itself. Without them, fighters are just brutes and fight-goers merely voyeurs and fights no better than street brawls: crude and amoral. Such is the significance of ritual in human history. So I moved my arms about a bit and rolled my head from side to side and shuffled back and forth and did all the things one does during a prefight staredown. But I was just playacting out of a sense of aesthetic propriety. Bliss was my domain.

But despite what the Buddhist poets may say, even bliss is a transitory state. And after the bell rang, mine lasted for exactly nine seconds. It was at that point that all that nervous energy my opponent had been carrying around all day came bursting out of him in the form of a hard jab and a cross that landed right on my chin. *So that's what it feels like to get punched in the face for real.* But before I could fully process the reality that another human being had just hit me, Jon was grabbing onto me, thrusting me backward violently, and pinning my body up against the cage. He had used those first two punches as a distraction to set up his takedown attempt. A classic MMA con, and I had fallen for it.

With my back stuck against the fence I felt right away how much stronger he was than me. I squirmed and shifted my weight and tried to get my arms under his, but I couldn't find a way to remove myself from his grip. With all the force of his weight Jon pressed up against me, the top of his head grinding into my jaw cruelly, both his arms dug in beneath my armpits to pin me back and squeeze the life out of me.

Suddenly he freed his right hand from my grip, reached back, and punched me clean in the face with a jolting shot—*pop!* I heard the crowd groan, and my upper lip immediately began to swell, but the punch caused me more shock than pain. At such close range it's hard for a striker to get the leverage to throw with any real power. Plus, biochemistry was on my side. During moments of stress and panic the brain releases chemicals called endocannabinoids and opioids to deaden pain. Fighters are blessed, like converts in a baptism, by a chemical analgesia, freeing them from the tyranny of physical suffering until the fight is over and the rush of adrenaline wears off. So I didn't feel much. Still, that punch was psychologically far worse than the two Jon had thrown to start the fight because it spoke of simple cruelty (no subtlety or sweet science in them) and of endless punches like it to come if I couldn't find a way to liberate myself.

All his years of college wrestling were conspiring against me, so the best I could do was keep him close, struggle when I could, throw as many knees as he did, keep one of his arms locked under mine in what mixed martial artists call an overhook, sit my hips back against the cage to deny him the leverage he needed to take me down, and try to mitigate any damage from his punches by moving my head from one side of my body to the other. If I let him take me to the ground I'd be in real trouble. The fight was only a minute old and I was entirely on the defensive. The fear I'd been expecting was not just upon me now, it was on the verge of swamping my senses.

But I wasn't scared for my health, or even my pride. No, what terrified me was the stalemate, the lack of action, the insignificance of what was unfolding. Yes, Jon was controlling me, but the fight had no movement or energy to it, no life. Despite his strength, he couldn't take me down, and I wasn't going to let go of his arms or keep my head static long enough to allow him to hit me with more than one punch at a time, so we sat there lodged against the cage, at an impasse. And precious seconds were ticking away. I was suddenly overcome with dread, not of bodily harm but of a scenario where bodily harm wasn't even a possibility. I worried for the first time that this fight might be a bloodless and bland affair and that my soul would be unchanged by the experience, which would be the worst of all possible fates, far worse than a concussion or a broken arm. And I began to feel offended at the thought that *this* could be the result of all those miserable hours in training, all those long subway rides on cold mornings, all those endless sparring sessions, all those missed bottles of whiskey and bland meals. Was this what I'd worked all those years for? Was this what I'd forced my wife through a year of fear and self-denial and self-obsession for? Was this what I'd dragged my friends two hours along the Long Island Expressway at rush hour for? *Could this be it?*

From somewhere nearby a voice shouted: *Knee, knee!* It was impossible to know whether the call was coming from my corner or Jon's. When the adrenal gland is flooding the bloodstream with epinephrine, it isn't uncommon to experience auditory exclusion, or "tunnel hearing." Unsure whose coach was shouting, Jon and I both responded by throwing knees, he to my inner thigh, me to his stomach. This difference in target would become relevant soon, but in the moment our actions didn't change anything. He still had me pressed against the cage and I still couldn't shake myself free. This seemed to be the nature of our relationship.

My greatest fear was being realized, and I couldn't do anything about it. My grappling skills were too limited and his strength was too great. My soul began to howl inside me at the thought that this was all my most ardent and ravenous stab at life was coming to. And the writer inside me (alive and aware even in those moments of pure physicality: like Christopher Isherwood, a camera with its shutter open, but under siege) rebelled at the thought that I would have to find a way to translate something so hideously dull, so devoid of magic and life, into words. To think of all that creative energy in service of such nothing, all those wasted words and thoughts, like seeds dropped on arid soil. My mad grasp for something meaningful was quickly turning into something insignificant, devoid of passion and narrative. The whole affair offended my aesthetic sensibilities and thumbed its nose at my desire for grand experience.

Then, from out of nowhere: a miracle.

In my agitation and anxiety, in my colossal impotent fury, in the general chaos and confusion of the moment, I had forgotten that a referee can break apart two fighters in the clinch if he feels the aggressor isn't doing enough to improve his position or mount an effective attack: if the fight has come to a standstill, which ours surely had. I was convinced I was doomed to be pressed up against the cage for the next nine minutes—portioned out in three three-minute rounds of monotonous misery with one-minute intermissions between them filled with self-doubt and hopeless pleadings from Thiago to free myself from Jon's grasp and get myself off that cage—and that there was nothing to be done about it, like a prisoner resigned to his sentence or a religious soul capitulating to God's judgment. But no, at exactly the two-minute mark of the fight, here was an authority as great as those offering a reprieve: for the better enjoyment of the crowd, sure, who hadn't paid eighty dollars to watch two men frozen in each other's arms for ten minutes, but just as much for my soul. If only the referee could have known what a gift he was giving me in that moment.

The referee pushed us apart and directed us back to the center of the cage to resume fighting. (Had it really only been two minutes? Another side effect of all that dopamine and norepinephrine is the distortion of time called tachypsychia, from the Greek for "fast consciousness." The mind is moving so quickly, the outside world slows down. Two minutes becomes an eternity.) Free from Jon's grip, I took a deep breath. Later I would learn that my friends saw this and assumed I was exhausted, but I was just breathing in the sweet air of liberation and possibility: like a death-row inmate after a last-minute call from the governor. The deep calm I'd felt before the fight was coming back to me. Jon, meanwhile, was starting to look tired. He was showing the slightly lowered fists and slightly open mouth that give the game away.

This is the downside of the body's enlivening fight-or-flight response: In the first minutes of a fight, adrenal glands flood the brain with epinephrine, amplifying muscle strength, speed, coordination, and focus, making the body stronger and less vulnerable to pain and fatigue. But all that amplification requires fuel. And once the initial burst of epinephrine wears off, the body finds that it's used up much of the glucose it needs for energy, leaving it drained and exhausted. Fighters who looked like champions for the first ninety seconds of a fight are suddenly overwhelmed with lethargy. Where before they were going mad with kicks and punches, now they can barely raise their arms or stand. This first-round collapse, known in the fighting world as an adrenaline dump, is common among newcomers.

Pressing up against another person with all your strength and trying to take him down is also exhausting, and I knew then that the subtle work I'd done in the clinch had paid off. The knees Jon had thrown at my thighs may have looked bad, but I hadn't felt them: too many cannabinoids and opioids rushing through my brain for that. In fact, it wouldn't be until hours later, when I was back in Brooklyn and could barely walk the thirty feet from my car to the front door of the bar, that those knees had their effect, long after the adrenaline had worn off. But while he had been throwing his knees to my legs I had been throwing my counter-knees to his stomach. They weren't big shots, and likely the judges didn't even notice them, but I knew those knees would eventually work their cruel magic on Jon's stamina. Body shots are precious commodities in fighting. Not as thrilling as head shots, not as celebrated in the eyes of casual fight fans or action-movie directors, but effective. A punch to the face will agitate, but a knee to the body will suck the air and the desire to fight right out of a person. And no amount of adrenaline can compensate.

We were back to boxing now, and I felt I had arrived at last in my world. After all those endless sparring sessions at Gleason's Gym, moving from one partner to the next, trying to make contact with the heads of all those shifting, slipping, parrying opponents, I felt overprepared to box with a wrestler struggling through the first stages of exhaustion. Jon was a great fighter, but trading punches with him wasn't nearly the same existential and aesthetic crisis as boxing Dorrius, who had devoted half a century of life to the art of not getting hit. Jon didn't move his head or counter or shift or slip, the way boxers do instinctively. Sensing this, I was now able to relax and fight as myself. My identity as a fighter could now be shown to the world, far from the paralysis of the clinch.

I started to throw my jab. The sweet jab that kept me going after I broke my right hand, that gave me purpose at my lowest moment, that I'd spent hours working while my right hand lay useless on my chin, was now redeeming me from the emotional quicksand of a grappling match. The jab would keep him away and off me. I heard Dorrius in my head, repeating his mantra like a song: *Just touch him! Just touch him! Just touch him!* So I touched him, with punches thrown almost without passion or intention, just little feelers, designed to distract and open up opportunities and holes in Jon's defense. I followed those jabs with a solid leg kick that landed on his outer left thigh—my first real shot of the fight—and saw him buckle a bit. He responded by charging

in with that same raging one-two combination he'd gotten me
with at the beginning of the fight, the one he'd used to cover his
takedown attempt, but this time I got my hands up in time to
defend and he didn't follow his shots up with a clinch. He was
too tired for that. The time for that was past. I felt emboldened
by the realization, free to do what I wanted. So I went back to
throwing my jab. One, two, three, four times. Nothing flashy
or even intimidating. None of them landed, but they kept Jon
moving backward and allowed me to establish the distance and
move him around the cage, to be in control: a welcome change
from the previous two minutes of powerlessness and paralysis.
Jon caught me on the chin with a jab of his own, but I didn't
mind. I was beyond the tyranny of the body by then, unmoved
by its concerns. As long as we were boxing, I was transubstantial: more spirit than flesh. We traded more jabs to the face and
I punched him in his stomach, aiming to chip away more at his
body and his will.

I was starting to feel comfortable in a cage, under all those
lights, half-naked and the center of attention. The fear of the
crowd and my opponent had drifted away, as had the frustration
of the clinch. I had no delusions about the effect my punches
were having—I hadn't hurt him in any meaningful way—nor
did I think I was winning the fight. No doubt the judges would
be scoring the round for Jon after all that time he'd spent manhandling me against the cage. But I was at peace. I started to
move my head a bit more and remembered the joy of faking and
feinting and my admiration for the subtleties of footwork. The
pleasure of fighting was coming back to me, beyond the simple
animal survivalism of those first two minutes. Just touch him.
Just touch him.

With twenty-four seconds left in the round I threw two
quick jabs, the first of which moved me into range, the second

of which landed square on Jon's nose, sending his head backward, and I felt a small explosion of delight go off in my brain, the same feeling I get when a sentence snaps into place on the page, only better. I had practiced the double jab over and over with my coaches, and here it was working. For the first time, I felt like a real fighter. There was no trace of fear now, no striving, even—just the thrilling realization that a technique studied and repeated over and over had done what it was designed to do. All that training, all that self-denial, all that discipline had *meant* something.

Was it my imagination or did Jon seem tentative now? Had that double jab sent a signal to him about my abilities? About his? Had that second jab, the one that actually landed, rattled him? After dominating me for two minutes but failing to get me down to the ground, had his confidence been drained away, smothered by his exhaustion and my stubbornness and sliced up by one stinging jab? A punch to the nose, no matter how light, can be disorienting, even humiliating, causing tears to fill your eyes and your head to move instinctively backward. The fear of a punch to the nose, that most exposed part of the face, is primordial. Your whole body screams in rebellion against that kind of vulnerability and rushes to protect itself. Did I sense that in him now? He seemed to retreat almost imperceptibly after that second jab landed. His body language hinted for the first time at confusion and concern. Did he recognize my newfound air of purpose and bliss? Or was I fooling myself? Was I allowing myself to get lost in the aesthetic thrill of a single successful combination? If so, was I setting myself up for catastrophe? Did it matter?

I threw another double jab (why not?), though this one was interrupted by Jon's punch to my body, which just barely grazed my chest but threw off my timing. No matter. Try again. Just touch him. Just touch him. Jon stepped back an inch while I pumped my fists a few times and shimmied my head to fluster him. Before, my head had been an unmoving target, begging to get hit. But I was loosening up now. We were outside each other's punching range, but constant movement will confuse an opponent and open up opportunities, and a head shifting continuously off the center line is much harder to hit. Once again I threw my double jab, stepping in behind the first punch to get closer into range, and then followed it up with a winging right, which flew right over Jon's outstretched jab hand and caught him on the left side of his jaw, where it meets the ear. *Pop!* It was the first cross I'd landed, proof that my efforts to open up his defenses were working and that Dorrius's lectures about the value of the double-jab-cross combination had gotten through. I let myself revel in the moment. That was a true punch. Not a jab, a punch. Like something from a schoolyard or a bar brawl: undeniable in its intention and brutality. Something animalistic and cruel. At long last I had hit someone.

But even in that moment of delight I knew Jon would be aiming to get that point back and get revenge for the pain I'd caused, so I quickly covered up my head with my hands and stepped back out of punching range and waited for his counterpunches to come back at me. But for some reason they didn't come. I pulled my hands back from my face and saw Jon lying facedown on the mat. Then I noticed the referee leaping in between us and pushing me backward. I looked to my right and my coach was leaping up and down outside the cage and pumping his fists in the air. I looked behind him and my friends were howling like beasts, crazed with joy. The rest of the crowd was howling as well. The fight was over. Jon had been knocked out.

I had knocked him out. I threw up my hands in disbelief and let out a huge breath. Who would have thought such a thing was possible?

It's a bit of romance that knockouts are all about power, that one good shot landing square on the nose will blast an opponent into unconsciousness—romance straight off the cover of a comic book. Our hero leans back and with all his might throws a colossal American cross and down goes the supervillain, or the Nazi, or the bullying brute. Justice is served.

It happens, of course. Some people are blessed with that kind of mysterious power or cursed with that kind of nose. But knockouts are generally more about placement and surprise than simple strength, more about fakes and feints and misdirection and deception and combinations and an accumulation of moves and countermoves that conspire to throw the victim off the scent of a knockout blow. Too busy responding to a distracting shot, the victim often doesn't even see this blow coming. And it's a truth universally acknowledged that it's the punch you don't see that knocks you out.

If I just threw power shots, not only would they likely never land, Jon would have been able to time them and shoot in on me as I was throwing them, making it easy for him to take me down. With my long arms and boxing knowledge, I had decided the distracting jab was my best hope, both for keeping a determined wrestler at bay and for creating the openings I would need to have a chance at a knockout.

So when I threw that first jab, its purpose wasn't to harm but to allow me to move into range and force Jon into a defensive posture, from which it would be harder for him to initiate an attack of his own. Just as I hoped, he pulled his head back to his right in involuntary response and went back a bit on his heels just as I was throwing my second jab. Neither punch landed, but they threw off Jon's movement, balance, and intentions. By the time he started to throw his own counterjab (on the video you can hear his corner calling out for him to throw his "1–2" combination just before this exchange), I was already throwing the overhand right that would precipitate the end of the fight. I brought this right hand over the top of his outstretched jab hand just as he was bringing his own head back onto the center line and caught him right under the ear. By moving his head in the direction of my incoming cross he unknowingly created a collision that doubled the force of my punch—like the accumulated power of two cars crashing into each other headfirst. Making matters worse for him, I had, quite unintentionally and perilously, dropped my right hand from my chin to my midsection as I made my move toward him, which allowed me to disguise the cross. And that's what did it: the distraction of those first two quick jabs followed by a cross that came up from hip level and was hidden from him by his own left shoulder. No great power or heroism—he just never saw the punch coming. Watching the knockout in slow motion, it barely even looks like I got him. But the most vulnerable moment in a fighter's life is when he's throwing punches. We're most exposed when we're trying. What a cruel metaphor fighting is.

Any list of the greatest knockouts of all time would have to include Muhammad Ali's impossible toppling of George Foreman in Kinshasa, Zaire; Holly Holm's shocking 2015 head kick that buried the myth of women's MMA pioneer Ronda Rousey's indestructibility; and the victory of the shepherd boy David over the great Philistine warrior Goliath in the Valley of Elah. But the greatest knockout of them all might be the one Rocky Marciano scored on Jersey Joe Walcott on September 23, 1952, to win the world heavyweight boxing championship. Walcott was considered an old man when he fought Marciano, way past his prime. He was thirty-eight, two years younger than I was when I walked into the cage. Marciano was twenty-nine, a year older than Jon Potts. Marciano, not a quarter of the boxer Walcott was but blessed with Homeric power and the gall of youth, based his strategy on wearing the older man down over fifteen rounds, suffering all the champion's maddening evasions, feints, baits, shoulder rolls, and subtle footwork—all the guile and cunning and wisdom of age—in order to get inside, batter his body, and land one of his legendary winging "blind" right hands. By the thirteenth round, though, Walcott had taken all the challenger had to offer and was still ahead on the judges' scorecards, and his footwork and head movement and counterpunching were flummoxing Marciano. With less than a minute left to go in the round, the frustrated challenger once again backed the champion up against the ropes as he had throughout the fight, feinted his jab a couple of times as he nudged in closer, and caught Jersey Joe with a terrific short right to the chin. Marciano's punch was colossal and horrible and Walcott's face had turned right into it, doubling the impact. Walcott slumped against the ropes and over a dreadful five seconds crumpled unconscious to the canvas, so slowly he seemed to be denying the pull of gravity. It was like watching a man getting sucked slowly into quicksand, never to rise again. No knockout ever captured so perfectly the aesthetic wonder and moral horror of prizefighting.

For all our enduring fascination with knockouts, we still don't know exactly what causes them. Doctors and other experts, searching in vain for an accurate anatomical assessment, often rely on the language of machinery, the clichés and metaphors of mechanics, to explain the phenomenon: the brain short-circuited, it lost power, the lights went out.

And they speculate. Some believe a knockout blow stimulates an overwhelming number of neurotransmitters to fire in the brain at the same time, overloading the nervous system, sending it into a state of temporary paralysis. Others contend that synapses in the brain actually disconnect as a result of the twisting of the brain inside the skull. Some argue that a solid hit to the jaw disrupts the reflex area of the carotid artery, which regulates the flow of blood and oxygen to the brain.

One ring doctor I spoke to wonders if the loss of consciousness from a straight punch isn't caused simply by the transmission of force through the jaw into the brain stem. Or maybe the rotational force from a hook or a roundhouse kick twists the stem or causes the brain to shear across the edges of the skull. Perhaps that force stimulates the trigeminal nerve (the largest and most complex of the twelve cranial nerves), causing a drop in heart rate, dilation of peripheral blood vessels, and constriction of cerebral blood vessels, resulting in a sudden loss of blood flow to the brain and unconsciousness.

My knockout blow landed right at the spot on the face that ring doctors, boxing trainers, and fighting theorists point to as the body's most vulnerable: the temporomandibular joint, where the jaw connects to the skull right in front of the ear. This spot is coveted and pined after and dreamed of in the fighting world. A punch there doesn't need to be thrown with overwhelming force if it lands just right.

As soon as mine did, Jon's legs gave out beneath him and he collapsed to the floor like a tent with its stakes pulled out. He dropped to his right knee, then his backside, and finally twisted over onto his face, his left hand posted out instinctually on the ground but powerless to stop his collapse. It was as if, to employ another fighting cliché, his switch had been flipped. By the time the referee jumped between us, though, Jon was once again in control of his body, lifting himself back to his knees and slapping the ground in frustration. The whole sequence took less than five seconds.

Doctors believe the sudden loss of muscle strength called traumatic atony may be caused by the momentary disruption of the vestibular and proprioceptive areas of the central nervous system and a sudden loss of motor control. The victim usually doesn't suffer any serious injury or concussion and recovers quickly. Which means the flash knockout is everything a civilized, conflicted, philosophic soul like me could hope for from a fight-ending punch: beauty without cruelty, paralysis without pain.

In Leonard Gardner's 1969 novel *Fat City*, boxing trainer Ruben Luna tells the young hopeful Ernie Munger after seeing him spar for the first time, "You got a good left. Step in with that jab. Get your body behind it. Bing! Understand what I mean? You hit him with that jab his head's going back, so you step in— understand what I mean?—hit him again, throw the right. Bing! Relax, keep moving, lay it in there, bing, bing. Keep it out there working for you. Then feint the left, throw the right. Bing! Understand what I mean? Jab and feint, you keep him off balance. Feinting. You make your openings and step in. Bing, bing, whop! Understand what I mean?"

I do now. It means through a few distracting jabs and a simple cross I can trace a line from myself to Rocky Marciano and Gentleman John Jackson and Ernie Munger and a whole glorious legacy of violence, and that in my own small way I'm living proof of one of the great scientific and aesthetic truths of fighting: the timeless, evergreen value of the simplest combination. What a thrill to feel connected through personal action to that kind of history, what enormous aesthetic, even poetic, weight it grants to my meager achievement. That three-punch combination, thrown out of habit and in the throes of ecstatic exhaustion, rings with the weight of fighting tradition and literary truth. Leonard Gardner. Jersey Joe Walcott. Fighting and writing, the twin loves of my life, together at last in one perfect moment. Sublime words describing sweet science, simple anatomy, and simplest mathematics. Jab-jab-cross. 1–1–2. Bing, bing, *whop!*

12.

ON THE WIRE

(ONE MONTH AFTER)

My life as an MMA writer began nearly a decade ago at a converted basketball gym in central Austin. For months I'd been watching fights at home alone, letting myself be seduced in secret, but I was terrified by what I'd find at a live event. Close up and free of the desensitizing filter of the television, would cage fights be too much to bear? Would my newfound interest in violence survive the transition from the Internet to real life, with its crowds and noise and actual blood?

The main event that night featured two young Mexican-American fighters, one from East Austin, the other from San Antonio, eighty miles to the south. I don't remember their names now, and most likely their careers never went anywhere, but their fight that night was such an unfiltered display of violence in all its beauty and barbarity that I can never forget it. It was as if it had been arranged to test the depth of my new affection. For fifteen minutes they attacked each other with such fury and abandon and passion that no one could have been unmoved by the experience or remained impartial. It could engender only adoration or disgust.

By the last round of the fight the two men were covered in blood and heaving great breaths, but still they fought on, as if their lives depended on it. And as the fight entered its final minute the crowd began to cheer them on as if *their* lives depended on it. The barrier between the two men and between them and the audience seemed to be melting away. The fighters *were* the crowd; their pain and triumph belonged to them as well.

In the makeshift press box twenty feet from the cage, even my fellow journalists and I fell victim to the overwhelming emotional pull of the moment. We couldn't help ourselves. How could we *not* rise to our feet to applaud what we were witnessing? What human being, even a human being as occupationally cynical as a sportswriter, could fight off the impulse to stand up and pay tribute and be a part of such a display of generous humanity, to breathe it in and connect himself to it? How many of those moments can one expect to be a part of in one life?

Walt Whitman, our prophet of communal transcendence and the interconnectedness of disparate souls, recognized this transformative power fighting has. In "A Song of Joys," the poet, so consumed with a desire for more life beyond judgment and morality that even the sight of a house on fire "maddens [him] with pleasure," praises "the joy of the strong-brawn'd fighter, towering in the arena, in perfect condition, conscious of power, thirsting to meet his opponent." Even the lowly, brutish fighter, Whitman writes, is part of the "vast elemental sympathy which only the human Soul is capable of generating and emitting in steady and limitless floods." Perhaps the lowly, brutish fighter most of all.

That night in Austin gave me my first sense of Whitman's elemental sympathy, of the undeniable thrust of particular moments to overwhelm both individual identity and will, of the transcendental power of a great communal force. I was sure my thirty-three years in America as a stark solipsist, an uncompromising materialist, and a practiced skeptic had left me impervious to that kind of spiritual aspiration. But there I was: swept up by a cage fight.

As soon as I realized I had knocked out Jon Potts, a great calm washed over me, what I can only describe as a profound sense of oneness with the world. In that moment, and to my great surprise, I felt a sudden deep and passionate love for everyone and everything around me. I felt love for every member of the audience, for all the cocktail waitresses and bartenders, for the announcer with his long dreadlocked ponytail and the cameramen and the judges and the commentators. I felt love for all my fellow fighters in the dressing rooms downstairs still waiting to fight and for all their coaches and cornermen and for the doctors now treating my opponent on the other side of the cage. I felt love for everyone who had cheered for me and everyone who had hollered for my head. I felt love for the three cameramen taking my picture in the cage and the commentator whispering in my ear that he wanted to interview me as soon as the announcer read the official decision. I felt love for people passing by the arena on the street unaware of what was taking place inside and of the great love I was feeling for them. And most of all I felt love for Jon, lying there on the ground, my partner on the road to whatever bliss was now overwhelming me. Our souls were now bound together forever by a punch to the head. How strange that this sport designed around harming others had engendered in me what so many other, more peaceful, more compassionate activities never could: a sense of connection to my fellow man.

So this was what it was like to feel immersed in a moment, to experience the triumph of the metaphysical. This is what the poets and spiritualists were always going on about. There really was a soul alive in this devoted cynic! And all it took to wake it up was a willingness to risk the destruction of the body—to discover the soul *through* the body, like Walt Whitman! For the first time in my life I felt entirely undiminished and unchecked, unmitigated, untouched, beyond the reach of anxiety and self-awareness and even my own poisonous psychic influence to mar. *Behold, the body includes and is the meaning, the main concern, and includes and is the soul.*

I'd experienced meditative immersion before, while playing music or having sex, but its meaning had always vanished as soon as the moment was over: after the last notes had drifted away, after the last involuntary jolts of orgasm had subsided. The great religious, transcendent fervor always disappeared, replaced again by the bland self-consciousness of secular life. But not this time. This time bliss was generously extended. This time, and *only* this time, I was given the opportunity to bask in my awareness, to see the other side, like the invalid who comes back from the dead and swears he saw the great light. I got to experience, for that moment, all the ecstasy of a mind at rest, all the enlivening power of a body put to its most perfect use, all the euphoric communion of consciousness and righteous exhaustion.

And for that one moment, with the stage lights in my eyes and the sound of the crowd filling my ears, I felt liberated at last from the weight of history, mine and my people's and the world's. I was free from the dictates of my personality and my reputation, my self-awareness, all the burdens of the past and a life lived. I was cured of all the burdens of being a writer, a Jew, a coward, my dad's son, a human being plagued by anxiety and self-consciousness, and an American watching his country collapse around him. That this great liberation was precipitated by a single insane act that no one ever would have expected of me made it all the sweeter. I'd been freed by a great refusal of the self and of my history. How like an American.

Neuroscientists studying the brain scans of subjects in the midst of "self-transcendent experiences" have noted a decrease in activity in the posterior superior parietal lobe, the area of the brain that distinguishes between the self and the surrounding environment. When activity in this part of the brain decreases, the lines delineating the self from the outside world and the people in it seem to disappear, creating the sense that individual identity and ego have dissolved into something greater. Researchers have noted this "intense experience of unity" in soldiers at war and astronauts gazing at the earth from outer space. Mystics might call such an experience ecstasy: "'I' passes insensibly into a 'we.'"

Poets and philosophers during the Romantic era pined for the sublime, not just the beautiful. True sublimity, they argued, was something beyond mere beauty; it occurred when the subject became conscious of an overwhelming force beyond his meager power as a human being to hold off, a force capable of making him feel his insignificance. To reach the ecstasy of sublimity an experience had to inspire not just admiration but awe and terror. And only the observer willing to give himself over to that terror experienced freedom from the burden of the everyday world and the temporary enlightenment of the sublime.

On good days my teammates and I talk about fighting the way Wordsworth and Schopenhauer talked about the sublime. Like it's our one shot at enlightenment, at feeling alive, at liberation from perpetual anxieties, at the transcendence of the mundane, at something like the ecstatic. As long as we're willing to face the terror, the sublime is always a possibility.

So now what?

I had experienced high living and higher consciousness and a great communion with my fellow man, and felt the sensation of my soul awash in exhilaration . . . and how do you come back from that? How do you return to earth after scaling the great heights? How do you go from the triumph of the cage back to the real world, a world that doesn't shine or shimmer and has no deeper meaning or delight, that offers few chances at sublimity or ecstasy or transcendence? Can I stand the boredom of a quiet life now that that sublime moment has passed, now that my five minutes of enlightenment are over?

A few days after the fight, when I was still basking in the glory of my knockout, a teammate of mine who's been fighting professionally for a decade warned me that a post-victory comedown was inevitable, that fighting was rarefied living and life outside the cage had nothing to compare to it or compensate for it once it's over. The feeling couldn't last, he warned me. Depression was likely. He assured me this was the reason I would want to fight again.

And sure enough, over the next month I could feel the emptiness growing. As the thrill of the fight dissipated, the demands of the everyday world reasserted themselves. All that life and lust and violence and energy and purpose were replaced by a boundless and bottomless boredom. Old habits, set aside during the monastic lead-up to the fight, began to reinsinuate themselves.

But reverting back to drinking and dissipation wasn't just about reaffirming dormant habits. It was something bigger than that. I was trying to reconnect to something transcendent, to the ecstatic, trying to recapture that fleeting thing that was quickly drifting into the fog of my memory, to approximate the wild, high living and awakened consciousness of the cage—to get back *there*.

Carl Jung believed that addiction and drunkenness are "the equivalent, on a low level, of the spiritual thirst of our being for wholeness," that the drunken soul longs for something higher and more sublime but settles for an approximation through a distortion of the senses and an "unexpected state of consciousness" where "caution and timidity are gone and the earth and sky, the universe and everything in it that creeps and flies, revolves, rises, or falls, all become one." Carl, how well you understand my plight. How does one slink back into the blandness of the everyday when one has touched the heights of bliss, when one has become all? It turns out William James was right: my materialist's soul wanted to commune with the mystic consciousness all along.

Is this the fate I'm doomed to—mourning the sensation of that one peak until I die? Approximating my one moment of glory and connectedness through chemicals? Watching a ten-second video clip of the knockout on my phone over and over until I go blind or mad? Living in the gilded past while wallowing in the squalid present? Dreaming forever of those three enlightened minutes? Is it all downhill from here?

It's remarkable what can happen to the fighter's body in just a month. Directed toward celebration and contemplation rather than conflict, the belly softens, the arms thin, the chest recedes, the leg muscles shrink, the hard lines of definition disappear, the eyes lose their glow, the aggression wanes, the desire drifts:

taken together, the body loses its air of power and presence, as if it no longer takes up as much physical space in the world or mental space in the minds of those it encounters. After a month of heavy drinking and long hours at my writing desk broken up only occasionally by trips to the gym and the rare sparring session, all my mental and physical energy is directed inward. I feel less impressive, less imposing, less like someone who demands attention and needs to be reckoned with. That I was ever someone who demanded attention or needed to be reckoned with may be a figment of my romantic imagination, but that's just the point: my soul is no longer filled with my body, or my body with my soul. The intimate connection has been cut.

I wonder how my wife feels about the change. I can still remember the way she looked at me in the months before the fight, when there was barely an ounce of fat on me, marveling that this was the man she'd married: the cerebral, artistic, ironic writer who had transformed before her eyes into something primal and imposing. Now that my body is regressing back to its original state, I wonder if she misses what's gone, if my newly shrunken shoulders and receding chest disappoint her. Does she resent me for this transformation, this great collapse? I'm way too afraid to ask.

Maybe I should fight again. Surely I can get it all back if I do: the heightened awareness, the great lust for living, the love for my fellow man, the feeling of size and substance. They can be mine again. Poetry and mysticism and transcendence and sweet delight. The marriage of the soul and the body. I can get back there!

No, I can't. It's impossible. A second fight would be nothing but a fool's errand, the perfect letdown, a desperate attempt to get back something long gone. How could I ever re-create the aesthetic and narrative perfection of that first fight? What could a second fight offer that would be better than a first-round knockout? How could I put my loved ones through it all again? My wife wouldn't understand. My friends wouldn't make another long trip. There could be no surprise. The transcendence and sublimity and oneness wouldn't appear again. It could never be the religious moment it was. I'd be chasing a ghost.

"Life is being on the wire," the great tightrope walker Karl Wallenda once said. "Everything else is just waiting." In 1978, after fifty years as a high-wire artist, Wallenda was attempting to cross between the towers of the Condado Holiday Inn Hotel and the Flamboyan Hotel in San Juan, Puerto Rico, when several guy ropes along the wire gave way, causing him to lose his footing. Wallenda tried to sit down, but he lost his balance in the high winds and slipped off, plunging 121 feet to the parking lot below. He was seventy-three.

Pankration, the ancient precursor to modern-day mixed martial arts, took its name from the Greek word for "all powers." With its blend of boxing and wrestling, pankration was the toughest sport in a brutal age. Fights ended when one fighter surrendered, lost consciousness, or died. During one match in 564 BCE, champion Arrhachion of Philgaleia got caught in a chokehold and was about to slip into unconsciousness when he managed to wrench his opponent's left ankle out of its socket. The pain was too much for Arrhachion's opponent and he submitted. By the time the referee pulled Arrhachion from the chokehold, however, the champion was dead. The victory crown was placed on his corpse.

———

So the voices of reason plead with me: Don't do it. Don't fight again. Forget the discipline and the self-denial and the pain and the injuries and the risk and all the misery. Move on. Live out the rest of your days in peace and leisure, waiting for the inevitable ax to drop but no longer seeking it out. Retire undefeated, like Rocky Marciano and Floyd Mayweather Jr. and Jack "Napoleon of the Ring" McAuliffe before you. Terry Marsh (26–0–1) retired because he had epilepsy, Kim Ji-Won (16–0–2) to become a performer in the theater. Surely you can retire because you realize that a second fight would be a spiritual, emotional, and aesthetic disappointment.

So save yourself. Preserve your limbs and your pride. Spare yourself the aggravation. Spare your wife and your mother and your friends the fear. Get out with your brain intact and your body unbroken and your record unblemished. Retire as the 197th-ranked amateur welterweight in the American Northeast. That's the reasonable thing to do.

Exactly one month to the day after my fight in Long Island, I'm hitting the heavy bag aimlessly at Gleason's, tapping away without purpose, when David Lawrence, the seventy-year-old trainer and writer, comes over and asks me when my next fight is going to be. "I don't know, maybe never," I tell him with a shrug of my shoulders. "Right now I'm thinking the best thing to do is give up and go out on top." David, who, like me, didn't have his first fight until he was forty but who kept going long after he should have stopped, defying his coaches and his doctors and the athletic commissions and his wife and common sense and the logic of self-preservation, making a beast of himself into his fifties, sacrificing his brain for the sake of experience and out of a deeply held belief that death would begin if he ever stopped fighting, just laughs. "No!" he says, punching me on the arm. "Go out on the *bottom!*" He laughs again and walks away.

As I watch David limp back to his office and close the door behind him, I feel my heart filling with something like joy for the first time in weeks. It's as if a firework has gone off. Suddenly there's a sense of possibility again in my soul. *Go out on the bottom.* Of course! Why didn't I think of that? How silly I was to think I could do anything else. That I could turn my back on the possibility of ecstasy and transcendence and bliss as if I'd never touched them. And in the name of safety and responsibility, no less. Why am I holding on to my health and my perfect record at the expense of high experience, putting my life into a museum to be preserved, for it to ossify and rot?

No, I want to live! And nothing in this world is stronger proof of the desire for more life than fighting. It's a spit in the face of the most fundamental human truth and an absurd declaration of our refusal to believe, deep down, in our own mortality. We run and we jump and we push and we grab and we kick and we punch, and for what? A burst of endorphins? A moment of bliss? Temporary enlightenment? A fleeting belief in the mother of all fantasies: that this doesn't end? Fighting is the tragedy and joy of the human condition in one—the classic refusal to go gently, the belief in our own ability to deny, if just temporarily, death and despair's claim over us. For that one moment, we're free. *In the midst of death we are in life.*

And life is the only thing that matters. Winning and losing don't matter. Safety and preservation don't matter. The perfect storybook ending doesn't matter. The only things that matter are experience and possibility and grasping at sublimity. The only thing is life. And perfection isn't life. Retiring undefeated isn't life. Going out on top isn't life. *Imperfection* is life. Going again is life. Clumsy, stumbling, wild winging blows are life. Loss is life. Decay and dissolution and recovery and more dissolution are life. The collapse of the body and trying and failing and succeeding and desperate drunkenness and giving in to age and lashing out in provocation and in the end losing: that's life. Life is defiance! Defiance of decay, of fear, of limitations, of history, of societal decency and morality, of inheritance, of age, of paralysis, of social expectation and fixed personality and death—of what we are and what we inevitably will be. Life is fighting to the point of incapacity and humiliation and shame, and beyond. Life is glorious failure.

ACKNOWLEDGMENTS

While fighting and writing may seem like solitary activities, it took the help of many people to get me into and out of that cage and through this book in one piece, and I can't thank them enough.

First, to my agent, David Gernert, who saw the possibilities and believed from the first, and my editor, Denise Oswald. I don't know what good thing I did in a past life to deserve an editor who loves fighting as much as I do, but thank god I did it. I would also like to thank everyone at the Gernert Company and Ecco for their hard work in bringing this book into the world. Thanks as well to Sudhir Venkatesh, who saw what I couldn't and led me back to myself.

I would have been totally lost without the patient assistance of Dr. Michael Kelly, Lauren McGill at the Fitness Institute of Texas, Dr. Adron Harris and Dr. Michael Drew from the University of Texas at Austin Department of Neuroscience, David Yaden at the University of Pennsylvania Department of Psychology, and Mike Dolce, MMA nutritionist par excellence. Thank you all for repeating everything slowly and multiple times.

I owe everything to my coaches—profound and generous men who gave me the tools to keep myself alive. Dorrius Forde for teaching me the sweet science. Rafael "Sapo" Natal for showing me life inside the cage. Mario Marin for explaining the mysteries of the clinch. And Thiago Rela for having my back on fight night. I'm also deeply indebted to all my teammates and coaches at Gleason's Gym, the Renzo Gracie Academy, the Renzo Gracie Fight Academy, and Fit & Fearless, especially the Sunday morning sparring crew, the Brooklyn MMA team, and my original fight family in Austin: Dave, Amy, Jason, and Ryan. All the beatings I suffered at your hands made walking into a cage tolerable. Thanks as well to Matt Ruskin, whose experience and guidance helped keep me sane before, during, and after the fight.

This book would never have been possible without Christian Bazán, who convinced me to take my first Krav Maga class and changed my life.

Thank you to Eugene Perez and Tom Kilkenny at Triton Fights for giving me a chance, and to Sherry Shokouhi, who has kept my mind right for years.

I don't have enough space to properly thank all my friends, but you know who you are and what you mean to me. Particular thanks go out to those of you who traveled deep into Long Island on a frozen night in December to cheer me on. I'm sorry for putting you through that.

All my love goes to Mom, Ed, Shana, Sara, Asa, Max, and Sid the Kid, who have treated my fighting fixation with all the bemusement it deserves. And to my father, who no doubt would have done the same.

To Katchen, the love of my life and the girl of my dreams: thanks hardly seem like enough for what you put up with throughout this process. Just know that I wouldn't have been able to do any of it without you—not throw a single punch or write a single word.

And last but very much not least, I want to thank Jon Potts for joining me for one of the strangest and most profound experiences two people can have together. I don't have the words, Jon.